THE GYPSY SEASON

by
George Nickels

Ashley Books, Inc.
Port Washington, N. Y. 11050

THE GYPSY SEASON
© Copyright 1982 by George Nickels.

Library of Congress Number: 80-12821
ISBN: 0-87949-187-6

ASHLEY BOOKS, INC./ *Publishers*
Port Washington, New York 11050

Printed in the United States of America
First Edition

9 8 7 6 5 4 3 2 1

Library of Congress Cataloging in Publication Data:

NICKELS, GEORGE
    The gypsy season.

    1. Nickels, George. 2. Nickels, Angelo.
3. Gypsies—United States—Social life and customs.
4. Gypsies—United States—Biography. I. Title.
DX127.N52A34   1980   973'.0491497   80-12821
ISBN 0-87949-187-6

Dedicated to
Ann Nickels
for her unceasing encouragement
and to
my beloved people—
the Gypsies

CONTENTS

INTRODUCTION

As far back as lost civilizations and Atlantis, there have been Gypsies wandering the world. Gypsies are, by nature, a happy and peaceful people, freedom-loving, truly children of the earth.

Contrary to popular opinion, there are *no* Gypsy kings and no royalty. Neither are there elections of any kind. Instead, Gypsy leadership is a spontaneous, natural development, the same as in any community. There is always a person of strength, integrity and outgoing personality who is respected, trusted and looked to in times of adversity. While in some cultures this may be an elected or appointed official, in Gypsy society this leader is generally an elder or the head of a family. He is not necessarily the oldest person in the group, but he is considered by the community to be the wisest. No decision is made without him. My father, Angelo Nickels, was such a leader.

The legend of Gypsy kings evolved centuries ago. To understand this myth is to understand something of Gypsy life and history. During the eleventh century, Gypsies fled persecution in the Middle East. Trying to get to a promised land, a haven, they traveled throughout Europe. Because they were "different"—dark-skinned, dark-eyed, and speaking a strange language—they were feared by the Europeans and often greeted with hostility or violence. For safety, they kept on the move, traveling in caravans of wagons, usually about twenty-five families (perhaps four hundred people) banded together for protection.

Each caravan had a wagon master or spokesman. Often to gain permission to pass through a town or village, this wagon master would say he was a king or prince from Egypt. The Europeans accepted this story and opened the town gates for the "visiting royalty."

This story was also useful because Gypsies were commonly blamed for any mishap in the community they camped near. If a chicken was stolen or a child disappeared, it was immediately said to be the fault of the Gypsies. But a wagon master who claimed to be Egyptian royalty could frequently calm an angry mob of local citizens by promising to personally punish any Gypsy guilty of any wrongdoing.

The word *Gypsy* also came into being during this era of persecution and flight. *Gypsy* does not represent a single nationality, such as the words *French* or *German*, but instead is a derivation of *Egyptian*, which was shortened to *Gypso* and finally *Gypsy*, because it was assumed the earliest Gypsies came from Egypt, as indeed many of them claimed.

The Gypsy Season, however, is not a book of history or folklore. Instead, it is the true story of another time when Gypsies were fleeing persecution, this time persecution by one of their own, a renegade Gypsy with gangster tactics.

The Gypsy Season is about my father's courageous stand against that Gypsy traitor. It is also an account of our family's struggle for a Gypsy existence and of the joys shared, the pain endured, and the hardships conquered in that search. It is a story of Gypsy valor.

Chapter One

Kidnapping, murder, prejudice, persecution and flight. These were the hard facts of Gypsy life my father learned in his earliest years. He also learned self-reliance and strength, and how to use that strength wisely and compassionately.

Angelo Nickels was born in Kiev, Russia, in 1894. By the time he was five, he was living in a Gypsy camp in Serbia (now Yugoslavia) with his father, mother and younger brother. The encampment of wagons was set up in a grassy meadow near a small town. The farmer who owned the land had given the Gypsies permission to camp there, which they did peacefully and happily. Each day Angelo's father and the other men went into town to ply their trades as coppersmiths or tinkers. The women stayed in the camp, cooking, sewing and taking care of the children.

For two years all was well. But then one day, when all the men were in town, a band of thieves struck. These men raided the camp, stealing whatever money and valuables they could find. And when they rode off, they also carried with them the Gypsy women and children. Among them were Angelo, his little brother, and their mother, Sora.

The Gypsies considered any aliens to be "Arabian," and to the frightened women and children, the fierce-looking men, armed with knives and guns, fit the description. Actually they were from Manchuria, but robbed and plundered throughout this part of Europe. Traveling on horseback so they could go farther and faster than the cumbersome wagons, they took their captives to their hideout in another part of Serbia.

The leader, Rupa, a tall, ugly man with a face scarred from many fights, had taken a fancy to the beautiful, spirited Sora. Once at the hideout, he gave her a choice. She could either marry him or he would kill her two children. Having vowed to do all she could to keep her children alive in hopes that one day the family would be reunited, she agreed to marry him. For two years Sora lived as the wife of a roving bandit. She took advantage of his frequent absences on raids to tell her children stories of their father and their life in the encampment, hoping to keep their memories alive. Then a daughter was born to her and Rupa. One night he got drunk and jealously decided to kill her other children.

Grabbing a meat cleaver, he chased Angelo and his five-year-old brother. Because Angelo was nine and fast on his feet, he was able to elude the Manchurian chieftan and get away. But Rupa caught his brother and threw him against the wheel of a wagon, smashing his head and killing him. Angelo watched from his hiding place, paralyzed with horror, unable to help his brother.

Later, as Rupa slept, Angelo crept back to camp. He had determined to kill the man and was searching for a knife when the grief-stricken Sora found him. She begged him not to kill Rupa because then his followers would kill them. Instead, they decided to run away.

So with no money, no food, and no clothes but those they wore, Angelo, Sora and her baby stealthily left the camp. They decided to return to Kiev. There were family and friends there, or at least there had been when they left. And if Angelo's father were ever to find them, surely he too would seek help from friends there, Sora thought.

Rupa was a powerful man in the area they had to travel through and his men were searching everywhere for the runaways. Not only did Rupa want revenge, he wanted his daughter back. So the journey was dangerous as well as difficult. Always on the alert, Angelo, Sora and the baby walked miles each day, sleeping on the streets or alleys of villages or in ditches or bushes in the countryside. They scavenged for food, often begging for handouts and money. Always they were afraid Rupa and his men would find them. At last they reached Kiev.

But here too disappointment and hardship awaited them. The family and friends they had hoped to find were gone and there was no way to determine whether or not Angelo's father had been there. By this time Sora and Angelo were completely penniless and again had to resort to begging and bartering in order to survive. Even here they had to hide, still fearing the evil Rupa. But because beggars were disliked in Kiev and hounded out of the city, Angelo, Sora and the baby were soon on the move again. From city to city they traveled, always meeting the same hostility, always on the lookout for danger.

In order to eke out an existence, Angelo began to sell scrap metal and then taught himself to be a tinker. Finally, after saving a small amount of money, he decided they had to leave the country. He returned to Kiev and went to one of the foreign embassies there in order to get assistance. But he was laughed right out the door because of his age—he was only twelve.

Despondent, he sat on the front steps of the embassy and cried. As he sat there, a man came up the steps and stopped to talk to him. Angelo told him his troubles and the man, who was the consul-general of the embassy, promised to try and help him. Angelo offered him the only treasure he had, his father's watch, the one possession he and Sora had never sold or bartered. The consul-general was touched but would not accept the watch.

True to his promise, the consul-general was able to help Angelo, Sora and the baby leave Russia. For some time, however, they remained displaced persons, traveling through China and Japan. Finally they saved enough money for passage on a ship to Canada. Angelo was blessed with a remarkable mind and could learn to speak a language merely by spending a few weeks in that country. In the course of his travels so far, he had picked up more than ten languages. Now, on the two-week voyage to Canada, he learned English.

After spending six months in Canada, he and his mother and sister moved to the United States. They settled in New York City and although Angelo was only twelve, he worked and supported the family. When he was fifteen, Sora remarried. She and her new husband eventually had four children, one girl and three boys.

When Angelo was seventeen, he married Ruby. Theirs was an arranged marriage, Sora having bartered with Rista, Ruby's father, for the bride.

In 1918, the entire family moved to Chicago. During the summers they operated a palmistry stand and souvenir concession in White City Park. Eventually Angelo saved enough money to hire an investigating team to search Europe for his father. Even though much effort and money were invested, all that could be learned was that Angelo's father had spent the rest of his life searching for his lost family and had later died brokenhearted in Hungary.

But Angelo's early experiences of violence and flight, as horrible as they were, were not unique. In fact, every Gypsy lived with equally traumatic memories or with the stories told by their elders of persecution and harassment, of the days and nights that were far too long because they were lived through in fear. Angelo knew them too, the stories of how Gypsies through the years have been accused of theft, kidnapping, even murder and cannibalism.

On the baseless charge of cannibalism, forty-five Hungarian Gypsies were racked, beheaded, quartered and hanged in 1782. On another falsified charge of kidnapping, forty-seven German Gypsies were imprisoned in 1872. Many were hunted down like wild beasts. In one Rhemish principality, the trophies of a day's hunt were to include, among other human game, a Gypsy woman with her suckling child. Throughout much of Europe during the seventeenth century, for the slightest offenses, mostly prefabricated, Gypsies were treated as cattle, their faces branded with hot irons. In the year 1624, in Scotland, many were condemned to a public death. They were drowned in the sea simply because they were Gypsies. These persecuted Gypsies were to set an example for others who were warned to leave Scotland's shores forever.

The feverish hate for the gypsy did not lessen with the passing of two centuries. In 1929, in a village near the River Drau, Yugoslavia, another Gypsy tragedy would occur. For reasons yet unknown, fifty Gypsies, an entire tribe, were forcibly compelled to move from their winter quarters in a season when Gypsies settle in, abandoning nomadic habits. Against impossible weather conditions, they were halfway across the partially frozen River Drau when the ice gave way under their combined weight. The screaming Gypsies, along with their horses and carts, crashed through the all too thin ice, disappearing in the water.

But the newest reign of terror was doubly horrible to the Gypsies because it was caused by one of their own. Although Angelo found great joy with Ruby and their growing family, he never completely forgot the evil man who had brought fear and tragedy to his childhood. The loss of his father and brother, the uprooting of his family, and their fear-ridden flight through Europe left a scar deeply carved on him. Now, when he learned about the latest tyrant who was menacing the lives of his people, he thought again of the cruel Rupa. Angelo, like his fellow Gypsies, felt fear, but being a righteous man to the core, his anger at the injustices inflicted by the traitor was greater than his fear. He controlled his anger and waited. He had to. The Gypsy traitor had hired men from the underworld crime syndicates. Angelo knew the peaceful Gypsies were hardly a match for mobsters.

Chapter Two

As though it were yesterday, I can clearly remember the year 1925, when I was five. My family had been living in Chicago for several years. They had been good times, happy times. We Gypsies were a proud people, respected by our neighbors, content with honorable work.

Angelo worked as a coppersmith, an ancient Gypsy trade stemming back to biblical times and Babylonia. On one occasion, as I stood by admiring his work, he bent down and said, "George, take this finished coffee pot to Mr. Rubenstein's store. Here's a penny. We're partners, boy, you and me." He instilled a feeling of closeness within me. Gypsy men take great pride in their sons.

How I looked up to my idol. I loved my father dearly and I admired and respected him as well. He stood five feet, nine inches tall. To a five-year-old, he was a giant Gypsy. His eyes, like the dark of night, were set deep. Midnight black and curled at its ends, his mustache was a sharp contrast with his dazzling white teeth when he smiled. When he spoke his commands to us, they reflected his love and devotion. Despite his lack of formal education, he was a man wise in the ways of the world, his teacher being each day's experience.

We lived in a storefront house. My mother, Ruby, and grandmother, Sora, operated a character reading parlor, an *ofisa* as it's called, in the front room of the house, colorfully decorated in the Gypsy tradition. Directly behind was an oversized room in which we lived. Here we ate and slept and sang and learned. Life was lived in close proximity with each other. Being members of a minority class, material survival and saving money were more important to us than plush quarters.

While father busied himself with his coppersmith business, mother and Grandmother Sora, both beautiful with their long braided hair and the colorful scarves worn by married women, maintained the character reading room. Meanwhile, the five of us Nickels children enjoyed becoming Americanized with games such as stickball in our backyard. Yet despite our interest in things American, our family was a team unto ourselves. As Gypsy tradition had it, my father was the head of the family and his word was the final command. My mother, Ruby, in keeping with the feminine role, was expected to help earn a living. All Gypsies work, but the women are usually the ones out in the public's eye.

The summer months brought delightful change into our lives. Travel and variety are important parts of Gypsy culture. They love it and we were no exception. From mid-April until Labor Day, Ruby and Sora rented another store two miles away at White City Park, and elaborate amusement park complete with games, a fun house, a carrousel, food concessions and, of course, our character reading parlor. They came by the hundreds, the *gadjos* as we call them, all those who are not gypsies.

When a *gadjo* came into the parlor store to have his fortune told, he enjoyed the mystery which permeated the atmosphere. But a *gadjo* entering an *ofisa* to have his palm or tarot cards read who carried peanuts in their shells would promptly be tossed out. It was believed he carried cloaks of death with him, the peanut shells symbolizing coffins.

Grandmother Sora was especially endowed with the gift of prophecy. From miles around, people from all walks of life came to sit with her, listening intently to what the future held in store for them. We children would peep in from the back, watching the *gadjos'* expressions of amazement. When Ruby and Sora weren't busy with readings, they would sew the long, colorful Gypsy dresses which were the feminine mode of dress.

Our way of life was peaceful then but soon it was all to change. The contentment, the security of home and business would be reshaped by destiny in a different way. As a complacent family we were hardly ready for the turn of events, but as Gypsies with a nomadic heritage we would rise to the occasion. With Angelo as anchor the Nickels family would survive.

Chapter Three

Through the Gypsy communications grapevine, the news began to trickel in, bit by bit. Relatives and friends from New York, Philadelphia, Detroit and Cleveland sent their stories of the *yek-on-om-amaro*, one of our fellow Gypsies who was ruthlessly victimizing his own kind, Gypsy families, forcing them to leave their homes and flee to California, or even to leave the country.

"How can this be?" stormed a shocked Angelo. "Who is this mad dog who tortures his own people?"

The Gypsy traitor's notoriety grew and his encroachment deepened with each day. Friends wrote to tell us that some of their Gypsy neighbors had found their homes burnt to the ground. The renegade had used them as an example, blazing a warning to others who would defy his demands for protection money. Some of these people were seriously injured, others killed. The Gypsy traitor's craze for wealth had become overpowering. It was not at all surprising when he became associated with one of the underworld mob leaders. Out of this despicable bond came the inept title King of the Gypsies. The newspapers began to carry stories of the colorful Gypsy "King." He and his followers made good copy for the reporters. Bands of Gypsies were overtaken by the thugs, beaten and robbed. Even the women were not spared. Their gold earrings were pulled from their pierced ears, the lobes left bleeding. Fear and pain clutched the hearts of the American Gypsies.

When the news came that the Gypsy traitor's mob was infiltrating Chicago, threatening the Gypsies on our own home ground, the moment of decision had arrived for us. Although Angelo was reluctant to leave Chicago, wishing to stay and fight, as well as continue his business, he knew too that the other Gypsies in the area were of a peaceful nature and not yet ready to make a stand. So once more, as fate would have it, we would lead the nomadic lives of our ancestors. Gypsies were again being persecuted and forced to flee. Unlike the persecutions of centuries ago, the pain of this one was deeper, far more penetrating, for this time a Gypsy traitor was terrorizing the Gypsies. No one really knew why. It was just happening. Astrologically, as a people, the Gypsies are ruled by the planet Neptune; now its forces were delivering the worst possible adversity.

Freedom was uppermost in my father's mind. No renegade Gypsy was going to get his clutches on the Nickels family. Although some Gypsies were leaving for Mexico and Canada as possible escape havens, Angelo calculated we would be safer in California because there were even more Gypsies seeking refuge in that state. There would be a better chance for protection there, he thought, safety in numbers.

With a mixture of sadness and anticipation, we bade farewell to all our *gadjo* friends in Chicago. Herbert Wyfield, owner of the amusement park, stopped at the house to say good-bye as we were packing our belongings, tying them onto our old green Cadillac convertible. Attached to the car was an open, two-wheel trailer carrying supplies and a cooking stove—a far cry from the old horse-drawn, gaily painted wagons.

"Angelo, you and your family will always have a spot with us in the park. We love you, Gypsy. Have a safe trip, and when you've managed to iron out your difficulties, return. You hear, come back."

Angelo, a man of deep feeling, was touched by Wyfield's genuine concern. Holding back the tears, father commanded, "It is time to leave." He motioned to Sora and Ruby to get the children seated in the car. And we were off to California, packed in tightly, looking exactly like what we were, Gypsies on the move.

The trip lasted for several months. We would often meet other Gypsies along the way who were also on the run. Caravans of Gypsies pitched tents along the road, staying for three or four days, sometimes lingering a week in favored locations. After several weeks on the road, we finally came upon a caravan of California-bound Gypsies. They were hospitable and glad for Angelo's strength, as well as for the protection that increasing their number would afford. We decided to travel with them.

Because our caravan wasn't looking for added problems, the men always asked permission of landowners before pitching our tents on a campsite. Most *gadjo* farmers were kind and often would employ some of us for a few days' work. Traditionally, Gypsies are a superstitious lot. Never will they set up a camp within view of a cemetery. Later, however, we heard of one tribe en route to California who stopped late at night in Indiana. Exhausted from the day's journey, they quickly set up camp, unaware of their location. Then, by light of illuminated torches, to their dismay they discovered their site was but a whisper away from a cemetery. As quickly as they had set it up, they disassembled their camp for fear that the spirits from the graveyard would disrupt it and cast a shadow of failure on the rest of the journey. Gypsies also believe that bats are birds of the dead. If you catch one and cut off its head, you will become rich and no harm will befall you.

It took many months before all the Gypsies arrived in California and assembled in a huge, sprawling encampment. More than three hundred tents made the campground a magnificent sight. A virtual tent city created a festive atmosphere with its panorama of brightly colored tents. Some were solid in color, others were striped. What joy it was for the younger generation to live in such a circuslike environment with plenty of new playmates around. For the elders there was a feeling of security in the size of the camp's population, and there was camaraderie for all.

Many of the tents had patio areas with bright, fringed awnings. These patios were bordered with deep, narrow trenches, for Gypsies believed that such trenches would keep snakes from entering their dwellings. Some Gypsies fastened good luck charms to their main tent poles. There is also a Gypsy superstition that a main tent pole may never be shortened, for cutting it would result in the death of the head of the family. If a Gypsy acquires a new tent, wagon, home or other building, he and his family are not permitted to sleep there the first night. The honors must go to a stranger.

Gypsy women are quite versatile in making the interiors of their tents attractive and homelike. They furnish the tents with Persian rugs, brightly colored overstuffed pillows to sit and sleep on, and round tables without legs. Cherished possessions are samovars, large copper coffee urns heated by a charcoal burner. Kerosene lamps highlight the colorful ribbons strung end to end on the ceiling. Assembling and decorating a tent calls for a wealth of skills, including many traditionally passed down from one generation to the next.

Despite the picturesque setting and the pleasure of companionship, our stay was destined to be full of hardship and frustration. In their attempt to escape from the

Gypsy traitor's yoke, many in the encampment had had to dip into hard-earned savings. Work was scarce in California and the Gypsies were grossly underpaid in the jobs they were able to find. Some worked as tinkers, knife sharpeners, or bought and sold scrap metal. Our family, as many others, picked peaches, oranges and apples in local orchards for two cents a bushel. After a day of back-breaking labor under a red hot sun, our total pay was less than a dollar. But there was a saving grace. Mother Nature looked after us. There was an abundance of fruit, game in the woods, and fish in the streams. We did have plenty to eat.

Close by our camp were the vineyards where many of the Gypsies worked, side by side with their children. During those warm days and cooled-off evenings in September and October, the vineyards were a treat for the eye, acres and acres of crimson, gold, and white grapes swollen with juice. The vineyards were the scene of feverish activity as the pickers moved through the rows, plucking ripe grapes from the vines to supply the winemakers who would work day and night crushing the grapes, making the new year's wine. The fragrance of fermenting grapes mingled with that of aging wines to yield a heavy aroma which permeated the entire area. Remembering it is to smell it again.

Gypsy holidays and weddings are spectacular celebrations. Every so often, our routine would be blessedly interrupted by the gaiety of one or the other. There were also birthday parties, marked by feasts with barbecued meats and presents for the young. Gypsies believe that birthdays are feathers in the broad wings of time. And there were, above all, the simple enjoyments of camp life, dinners in front of an open fire, the sights, sounds, and smells of greenery and the sweet earth.

One of the greatest pleasures of this time was the story telling. The elders, who were really trying to remain awake, taking turns guarding the camp, would tell us stories about our ancestors and exchange among themselves Gypsy folklore. One story I heard then was about the crucifixion of Jesus Christ. The fourth nail, intended for his pure heart, was stolen away from the Roman soldiers by a Gypsy in order to save Jesus. Jesus knew this and forgave all Gypsies forevermore who are forced to steal to survive.

Because Romany is a spoken language, not one written, our heritage was transferred by word of mouth. Even as children we knew instinctively that we must remember what we heard, and we did. During those nights in California, when huge campfires were kept ablaze all through the night as a means of protection from the Gypsy traitor's marauders—the fires lit up the sky so if anyone was approaching the camp, they would be easily detected—we listened to the stories of our elders and learned of our history.

With the appearance of dawn's light, we would arise to the sound of meat sizzling in great round frying pans. To the Gypsy, watching the sky and all its glorious changes is like listening to a symphony of nature. We are told the stillness of morning whispers, "God is awakening." Blissfully unaware of our parents' burdens, we children in the camp eagerly greeted each new day. We enjoyed a carefree life of games, sightseeing and the small chores assigned to us. Gypsy children are often spoiled because at the age of twelve, they are considered adults and are expected to assume their share of responsibility. So, because their childhood is so short, they are indulged, protected, and treated with much affection by all the adults. And we in the camp were no exception.

There was one wise old Gypsy woman in the camp whom all the children came to love. She would tell us stories and teach us how to think. I can remember myself asking her once how to always be happy. "Don't allow the seeds to spoil the enjoyment of the watermelon, just spit them out," was her reply and she turned back to the small Gypsy children who had gathered around her and began telling them how water lilies are really fallen stars, and about the luck which is promised if you find a turtle carrying a blade of grass in its mouth.

Chapter Four

Providing desirable brides for their sons is an important task for Gypsy parents. A wise Gypsy father will tell his heirs to select a daughter-in-law with their ears, not their eyes, that the emphasis should be placed on a maiden's morals and character rather than physical beauty. A wife must help earn the family living so it is hoped she has intelligence, strength and other virtues of mind and soul, as well as body. Traditionally, much of the selection process occurs around the campfires where young Gypsy women are respectfully and carefully appraised. And in our tent city in California, the tradition continued.

Suddenly the camp came alive with gossip about Pete Cooper and how he had previously pledged his daughter

to the Gypsy traitor for his son. The pledge had been
made when the renegade was still a respectable Gypsy.
But then, in blatant contempt of age-old Gypsy custom,
the traitor had arrogantly taken the maiden Cooper away
by force, without payment of dowry. Pete's younger
daughter, Ann, had also been promised before the ab-
duction to the Gypsy traitor's other son. But as fate
would have it, while in the California camp my uncle,
the fourteen-year-old Frank Nickels, had fallen in love
with Ann. Pete Cooper knew this. Wanting his daughter
to be happy, he suggested to Grandmother Sora that she
attempt to bring the two of them together in marriage.
He approached Sora only because her husband was
dead. Usually all business transactions are negotiated between the men.

"But what about the Gypsy traitor? He wanted Ann
for his son. It is done. She was promised." Sora's look
was one of despair, her dark eyes seeming to search for a
way.

"Why be frightened of him, Sora? I'm not. He and
Chicago are far away now," protested Pete.

Finally convinced, Grandmother Sora agreed. She pro-
ceeded to appraise the seventeen-year-old Ann as Uncle
Frank's prospective bride, finding her to be more than
suitable for the hard struggle of Gypsy existence, and especially even-tempered. Sora was sure that Ann would
be a good worker. Even though good looks are a last
consideration, Ann was beautifully endowed. Pleased,
Sora hastened to make arrangements for what promised

to be the most elaborate, ritualistic Gypsy wedding in years, Uncle Frank and Ann's.

With the engagement practically assured and because so many relatives and friends of the bride and groom were arriving daily, it was decided by the leaders that we should break up the camp and relocate on a larger stretch of rented flatland. For three long days the hauling back and forth went on until, finally, we were in Sacramento, a glorious spot, one which we would forever remember.

Envision a huge bonfire blazing between two rows of multicolored tents, the odor of burning wood floating over the encampment on the breezes of a summer's eve, fireflies adding to the excitement. There, around the fire, a circle is formed. Half of it is made up of women, some of them sitting on rugs or eider down pillows, others on the ground. Men complete the other half of the circle. And so it was as the bargaining for the bride, Ann Cooper, began. Sora sat in the circle along with Pete Cooper and his wife, the bride-to-be's parents. Fortunately for Uncle Frank, Sora Nickels was a wealthy Gypsy, in an enviable position to bargain for the bride's price. Actually, Sora and the Coopers had already gotten together. Due to Sora's wealth, an unusually high bride price of $6,500 was offered. But despite the generous offer, tradition demanded that the ritual be acted out.

Actually, the haggling over dowry is a major part of the prewedding excitement. If a Gypsy parent is poor, when the wedding is over he may have lost what little he possessed, or even be forced to borrow from his friends. If the father-in-law is wealthy, he can be almost bankrupt by the time the dowry is settled. On rare occasions, if the marriage does not work out, the bride's father must return at least half the bride's price. Of course, there is some loss of respect attendant on this too.

As the bartering began, the men, including Pete Cooper and his sons, sided against the women, accusing them of trying to extract the last penny. There were even playful threats of calling the wedding off altogether. First one Gypsy, then another, would step to the center of the circle to be heard, as the haggling was an event open to all. There were many altercations and heated discussions and the haggling went on into the early morning hours. In all, it was a social ritual, an occasion for all to express their opinions.

The price eventually settled upon was $6,500, as had been earlier arranged. Sora would have to send to the bank for it. She was too shrewd a businesswoman to keep that amount of cash on hand. After these financial details were worked out, Sora politely asked the bride-to-be's mother if Sunday two weeks from then was suitable as a wedding date, and she agreed. Whenever possible, Gypsies try to marry on Sunday.

When her money arrived from the bank, on the Friday before the wedding, Sora sent word to the Coopers to call forth the witnesses. It is a Gypsy custom for the witnesses to count the bride's price, seeing to it that her family is not cheated. Pete Cooper invited six men to be witnesses. After they carefully counted the money, it was given to the bride's mother to count again. Once all the counting was over, a special bottle of the best available whiskey was set out.

The tradition is that the whiskey bottle is gaily wrapped with a bright red scarf entwined with a necklace of gold pieces. The scarf *must* be red. Then the bottle is passed around for all to sip, but it must not be emptied, for that would bring bad luck. The bottle, still partially filled, is given to the bride's mother along with the dowry. On the night of the wedding, the bride's mother places the chain around her daughter's neck. The morning after the marriage is consummated in a newly prepared wedding tent, the bride is expected to thoroughly wash herself, then tie the red scarf around her head before leaving the tent. Gypsies use the scarf as others use a wedding ring. No actual words or vows are exchanged.

Sora, with the assistance of my father, Angelo, was determined that we Gypsies would have a wedding feast to remember, festivities to blot out, if only for a few precious days, the threat of the Gypsy traitor in far-off Chicago. She had rented for the wedding a huge circus tent, the sides of which were left open, inviting the warm Sacramento climate to take part. She had also hired a Gypsy orchestra on a day-to-day basis. The length of wedding festivities is in accordance with the wealth of the groom's father or family, and Sora expected that the celebration of her son's wedding would last for at least a week, instead of the usual three or four days. Sora ordered quality foods in such quantity they could have rivaled a Roman feast. Meats, breads, and cheeses would arrive on a daily basis, as well as wine in ten-gallon jugs.

Several youngsters were sent out to scour the nearby woodlands for green wood to make the Y-shaped posts for a dozen spits. One of the blacksmiths in the camp made similar steel posts and wire links to hold the heavier pigs and calves which were to be roasted. Huge pits were dug in the ground and filled with charcoal and wood.

A flag was raised on every tent. The tables were decorated and California's flowers were everywhere, even banking parts of the rented circus tent. Liquor caches bulged with barrels of beer, brandy, whiskey, and assorted wines which ranged from the cheapest kind to the two- and three-year-old varieties. Gypsy seamstresses were working feverishly on Ann's white wedding gown, ingeniously weaving daisies and other floral designs through the fabric and the veiling. Clotheslines bloomed against the California foliage with magentas, blues, oranges, yellows, a virtual explosion of color as the women prepared their finest attire for the wedding. Men's printed satin blouses were made with heavily gathered sleeves which hung six inches deep and gripped the wrists snugly with ornate buttons.

Enterprising youngsters bored holes in the eight-foot-high fences that surrounded the encampment. Some removed parts of the boards here and there, announcing their intention of allowing Californians the privilege of

witnessing a real Gypsy wedding, along with its me-
lodious festivities, for a nominal fee of course, ten cents
to a quarter. One Gypsy prepared a long, ribbon-deco-
rated pole which was topped with good luck wedding
bells, the metal type from India. This was used to lead
the wedding procession.

Even as the encampment prepared for the celebration,
there was still time for stories, especially stories of other
weddings. One I especially remember was about a tribe
of Gypsies being pursued by soldiers. One of the fugi-
tives reminded the Gypsy leader that this was to have
been his wedding day. The leader stared at him in
amazement, then replied, "But we may all be dead in a
few hours!"

"All the more reason to have my wedding now," the
young man pleaded, and the leader smiled with an ap-
proving nod. When the soldiers arrived at the Gypsy
camp, they were greatly surprised. Instead of fleeing for
freedom and their lives, the Gypsies continued their
dancing and singing in celebration of the wedding. The
soldiers lowered their guns as the harmony had dissolved
their official intentions. Suddenly a dancing Gypsy girl
whirled by, taking an officer with her, then another followed, and another. In a moment they were all dancing,
Gypsies and soldiers together. And the very next thing
the soldiers knew, their guns were gone. They would
leave empty-handed while the Gypsies escaped. For not
only are Gypsies in love with celebrations, they are also
masterful at outmaneuvering their adversaries!

The wedding day arrived with all of the sun's glory blessing it. The festivities began. Sora motioned to the orchestra and beckoned for the crowd's attention. Then she took a very large loaf of bread and hollowed it out. She put gold and silver coins into the loaf, then poured salt, representing fertility and a full life, into it. As the bride and groom looked on, Angelo made the toast to the Pooranesto ("the old ones"), the ancient tribe all Gypsies, so the legend goes, are descended from.

"Frank, Ann, may this silver and gold bring you joy, happiness and health throughout your life together. Forever may you be as one."

Two Gypsies who had been chosen earlier then moved through the crowds to collect money from each man. One held the loaf, one carried scarves. Two men are used for this task so each will keep the other honest. As each man dropped his contribution, a ten- or fifty-dollar bill, into the bread, a new scarf was placed around his neck and the collector signaled to the orchestra to salute the gift giver. Then the filled loaf was presented to the bridal couple and the feasting began. Some time during the evening, the newlyweds retired to the bridal tent and the marriage was consummated.

All during the wedding feast, the huge trenches in the central clearing were filled with glowing, smoldering wood and charcoal. The Y-shaped posts on either side of the trenches held rods laden with as many as a dozen piglets, slowly cooking over red hot coals, sending forth mouth-watering smells, promising the tastes which were to come. Larger spits held the full-grown porkers, pigs weighing up to 110 pounds, sprinkled with just the right amount of aniseed. The Gypsy blacksmiths had done their work well, fashioning the sturdy iron spits to hold the heavier meats, sheep and half-flanks of beef. These were flavored with rosemary and cayenne pepper.

The children turned some of the smaller spits; tiny Gypsies, dark-eyed faces fixed with smiles, hands clapping, shouting with glee as the fat dripped into the fire which would then blaze up, threatening to reach them. Angelo and the other men were gathered around the larger spits, taking turns polishing the pigs by pouring ladlefuls of lard over them. Meanwhile, other children fed planks and aromatic herbs to the roaring fires. One old Gypsy joked, "You know, the pig would be my favorite bird if only it had wings." The odor of browning meat was tantalizing, as was the blending of spices and herbs. The fragrance was a potent and welcome appetizer and anyone could eat whenever he was hungry. The wedding feast was to stretch for eight long days and nights, a tribute to Sora's wealth and position, and testimony that, at heart, all Gypsies are as little children.

The women scuttled back and forth endlessly as they transported their buckets of water from the nearby spring. Big cast iron cooking cauldrons had been previously scoured for the big event. Swinging rhythmically now above the flames were round black kettles and cooking pans, hanging from their triangular supporting apparatus. Silvery steam issued from the pots, adding another delicious aroma to the already perfumed air. The women had earlier cleaned and prepared the vegetables, mounds of sweet peppers, lettuce, tomatoes, onions and cucumbers, and now they began to fry potatoes and boil cabbage leaves which would be filled with chopped meats, rice and laced with spices. Other delicacies were spiked with slivovitz, a liquor distilled from plums. The women also set out horseradishes, black olives, cold baked eggplants mixed with chopped raw onions, and meatballs flavored with nutmeg. There were also many kinds of beans, including the beet red variety which had become even darker from the paprika used as seasoning. Loaves of bread were piled into pyramids, high as a Gypsy tent. Trays were stacked high with flat, flaky Gypsy cakes, part bread and part pastry.

Since the liquid refreshments did not require any preparation to speak of, the adult Gypsy camp was well cheered long before the day's roasting was complete. The children were allowed to drink wine which was heavily diluted with grape, strawberry, or cherry soda. How the cheer spread as frothy beer flowed freely from the kegs, filling every possible container from cups to buckets! Wines, some mildly effervescent, were circulated in glasses, served from ornate copper trays. Most of the men were more receptive, though, to drinking right from the jugs. Others enjoyed specially prepared brandy, a unique product of Gypsy talent. Bottles are slipped over the flowering branches of pear and apricot trees so that the fruit will develop within the glass containers, reminding one of those hand-crafted ships in bottles. When the fruit is fully grown, perfectly ripened, the branch is cut close to the fruit. Brandy is then poured into the bottles and they are set aside for special occasions.

With wine going to everyone's head, the merry making grew louder and louder. By evening, campfires and lanterns made weird, giant, distorted shadows on canvas walls. Loud, sometimes rollicking laughter rang out, snatches of songs floated on the breeze, and brief quarrelling could even be heard periodically. Gypsies believe that once a note of music is played it will never fade away, but is absorbed in the ether of the universe, ready to return another day. Clapping hands, clicking castanets, mandolins, violins, guitars and tambourines blended in a wild concerto. Gypsy music is free, played as the feeling dictates, and to the musician it is second nature, as easy as breathing.

It is said that in some parts of the country *gadjos* call autumn the season of the Gypsy woman because it, too, is garbed in yellows and scarlets, with berries shining like rubies. And at the wedding dance, the hundreds of Gypsy women did indeed seem to personify autumn and its beauty through their colorful dresses and vivid dancing. As a Gypsy woman begins to dance, there's a spring to her prance, an enticing sway to her steps, livelier still if she's been to the cider keg. Even the older women seemed to forget their years during the festivity and energetically joined in the dance. There was movement everywhere, snapping fingers, clicking tongues, stamping feet, swirling skirts and shining black hair swinging wildly, highlighted by the flickering firelight. It was wild; it was beautiful. The women seemed to glow, their beauty enhanced by graceful skirts, satin blouses, velvet jackets adorned with golden bangles, rings and earrings.

Gypsy dancing, like Gypsy music, is spontaneous and improvised. As the music grew wilder, the shouts of the Gypsies grew louder. Almost barbaric, the scene was filled with an ecstasy of motion, the dancers spinning faster and faster until only the best, the strongest remained, whirling madly like tops.

Temporarily freed from an otherwise constant supervision, my brother and sisters and I had enjoyed the festivities to the fullest. Finally, exhausted from it all and stuffed with delicacies, we took shelter in our tent. Burying ourselves in the eider downs, we quickly fell asleep. As the dawn appeared, coals still smoldered. Lanterns too were still glowing through some of the tents, making them look like giant lamp shades, red or blue or striped. Circles of light were growing smaller and smaller and the fires were dying out as the grownups gradually withdrew to their tents and surrendered to sleep.

Chapter Five

From the earliest days of their culture, more than a thousand years before the birth of Christ, Gypsies had made it a practice to sacrifice horses and other animals on special occasions, including weddings. Frank and Ann's wedding party was in the sixth day of its festivities when we were reminded of this almost forgotten ancient custom. It had a dampening effect indeed.

A year before the wedding, the fourteen-year-old John Daniels (Gypsies are men by age fourteen) had displayed an amorous interest in Ann Cooper, now Mrs. Frank Nickels. But Ann had not returned his interest. Whether John had heard of the old custom and believed in it or whether he just wanted to stir up trouble was not clear. But stir up trouble he did. Suddenly from a distance, be-

hind the tents rose the roar of a crowd, shouting riot-
ously, screaming protests. Resembling the movement of
locusts, they swarmed into the open area.

Daniels, in the middle of the crowd, was leading a
horse that belonged to the bridegroom, Frank Nickels.
The animal was an old, worn-out bay who could hardly
keep its head from hanging limp. But now, because of
the flickering lights, and the noisy crowd with their emotions running rampant, the old horse rallied 'round with
a show of spirit, plunging and tugging at his halter.

"What the hell are you doing with my horse?" demanded Frank. He loved the animal.

"I'm doing your wedding up right and proper, lover
boy," said Daniels sarcastically. "May your old devil
scarificed bring you both luck." Someone seized the
bridegroom's arm from behind, pulling him back, away
from the horse. The crowd kept closing in, circling
around Daniels and the horse. Sora, realizing what was
about to happen, pulled Ann away as she tried to reach
Frank. Daniels, strutting around the poor beast like a
peacock, lifted the knife from his sheath and held it up
defiantly, allowing the sun's light to reflect from it.

With a backward sweep of his arm, he played with the
crowd, pretending to strike, and the crowd suddenly widened. Once again, Daniels stepped back. This time, with
the backward sweep of his arm, he thrust forward, throw-
ing himself on the animal, stabbing it over and over
again. The first stream of blood flowed from below the

shoulder, then from the throat. An eerie, overpowering silence fell on the crowd, broken only by the choked sobs of children and hushed words between the women. Then the horse fell heavily to the ground. From out of nowhere came a shot to the horse's head, putting him out of his misery. The ancient Gypsy custom was fulfilled—how unnecessary—but fulfilled nevertheless, and all hell broke loose.

Women scurried to get children out of the way. Daniels, covered with blood, knife still in his hand, remained in the center of the circle and was jumped by Angelo. A riot erupted. More than sixty Gypsies joined the fray, men and women. All the festivities of the past week were made a mockery of as blood spilled to the ground, accompanied by the sounds of crunching bones and cracking heads, clicking like castanets. Tents were torn to shreds, pillows ripped open, kettles and buckets overturned. It was a civil war, one clan of Gypsies divided among itself, with the women's barbarism causing most of the havoc. It was they who turned it into a bloody massacre. Gypsy men are intimidated when their women rush in. They are fearful of the angry women, more frightened of their most formidable weapon, those long file-pointed nails, than of the blows of other men, preferring a hard fist any day. As the women attacked, they shouted curses at their victims.

"May they stick and twist a knife in you that will act as a spike in your guts," screamed one.

"God grant you may get one hell of a fever, so that all your bones feel like they've been poured into boiling water," shrieked another.

"You Gypsy trash."

A fair fight is rarely the goal when Gypsy women are in combat. Winning is all that counts and they made this contest a free-for-all. There would be no fight left in them when the fisticuffs were over. Tent stakes, pieces of iron, anything they could lay their hands on were grabbed up and used. They also resorted to pulling handfuls of hair from one another's heads. Quick as lightning, they savagely hammered away at each other, blood-chilling screams piercing the otherwise glorious afternoon. One woman with a knife lunged at another, splitting her ear lobe. It hung limply, blood running down her neck. Her earring had been ripped from her ear. From this day on, many Gypsy women would carry slit ears as battle scars, a tribute to their participation in the horse melee.

It was as if the free-for-all provided a release for the pent-up emotions of the past months. With their inherited code of ethics, the Gypsy men kept at the fight. Through the scraping of their boots you could hear the thud of the blows. Despite the intensity of a Gypsy fight, it is seldom to the death. Never will a Gypsy hit a man when he is down. The victor simply leaves him, turning to find another opponent. With the exception of kicking and hitting below the belt, which no ethical Gypsy would resort to, there are no holds barred. A stand-up to the knock-down contest between two Gypsy men is an honor-bound event. There is a winner and there is a loser. When a fight is finished the ill-feelings are supposed to be set aside with it.

One of the peepers-for-a-quarter at this fight had called the police. Fearing the law's lack of understanding of Gypsy ways, some of the men tried to stop the brawling before they arrived, but to no avail. A Gypsy tigress intervened, jumping on, scratching and clinging to one of the men's backs, her feet locked tightly around his waist as she beat at his head. Finally he was able to throw her off. She grabbed a cooking pan and ferociously hurled it at him. He caught it on the forehead and fell, unconcious, to the ground. He was dead.

Word spread that the police were on their way. Thoughts and actions now turned toward self-preservation. The fight was over. One of the Gypsy men, a farm owner who lived in the nearby countryside and who worked as a deputy sheriff of the county, was participating in the wedding festivities. He was afraid to be caught with his guns, fearing his job would be in jeopardy. He knew he had to get rid of them in a hurry before the police arrived. Looking around, he saw me and my Uncle Bill, both of us eight years old, protecting our hides beneath a table which had been set up for the festivities. He commanded us to come out and ordered us to hide his guns until after the police left.

In the midst of all the confusion, Uncle Bill and I placed the gunbelt with its guns still holstered in a bag and slipped out of the camp unseen. We ran for a beach that bordered a lake near the camp. Frantically we dug a hole for the guns, not yet realizing there was a fisherman seventy-five feet to the left of us. Just as we were placing a stick in the loosened earth, marking it for our return, we saw the fisherman and noticed he had landed a beauty. We should have realized then that fisherman had peripheral vision, but we didn't. All the time he was fishing, he was taking in our actions. When we arrived back at the camp, the area was crawling with police and the ambulance had also arrived. The cops were facing an impossible task as Gypsy after Gypsy was questioned.

"Who knows what happened? Who started this havoc?

"Who killed this Gypsy, which one of you? Look at the poor bastard. Who?

"Doesn't any one of you know what went on here?"

"Jesus, look at the horse," said another sickened cop.

The Gypsies simply stood there, many of them with their eyes looking like rotting cherries, their clothing torn but staunchly in unison once more. In despair at the lack of cooperation, the police withdrew from the camp. The dead Gypsy was carted away in the ambulance, his polka dot scarf thrown of top of him.

When the wife of the dead Gypsy, Milano, returned from telling fortunes in a neighboring town (no one knew why she wasn't at the wedding feast) to find out her husband had been killed, she became wide-eyed, looking for a reason, looking wildly all about her for the killer. Then she went berserk. She grabbed a can of kerosene and began sprinkling it on the tents. One of the women with but the flicker of her eye had told the screaming wife which side of the clan was responsible for her husband's death. Realizing that Milano's wife was temporarily insane and that in a way each was responsible for his death, no one made any attempt to stop her. The woman who had actually hurled the pan that killed Milano was being guarded closely by her family.

Then, as tent after tent caught fire, smoke and flames reached high in the sky. Only rubble and ashes remained of the belongings of the Daniels side. One grief-stricken Gypsy woman had finished what Daniels had begun. Several Gypsy men took it upon themselves to bury the horse, right there where the poor beast had died. Frank and Ann walked alone to the far end of the camp. Another family took Milano's widow in to help her make his funeral arrangements.

With the dawn of the next day, Uncle Bill and I rushed back to the beach to recover the guns we had buried. But of course they were gone. No doubt the fisherman went home with more than just the day's catch. We were frantic, fearing the Gypsy sheriff would beat the life out of us. How were we to explain away the loss? "Do you suppose he'll forget he gave us the guns, Uncle Bill? There are lots of kids in the camp, will he remember us?" I asked naively. We went back to the camp and tried to keep out of sight. After several days had gone by and neither one of us had been approached, I realized my wish had come true.

Chapter Six

Gypsies are buried according to their specific requests made while they are still alive. If a Gypsy has a premonition of death or knows he is on his deathbed, he will tell those around him the exact arrangements he desires. Gypsies believe a man should die in peace, knowing his wishes will be carried out. In Milano's case, despite the fact that he wasn't able to give directions for his funeral, he had been wealthy so many orchestras were hired to play at his wake. For three nights and three days, as custom would have it, the doors of the funeral parlor never closed as Gypsies filed in to take their turns staying with his corpse and paying their respects to Milano's widow and family. A Gypsy's body must never be left alone until it is buried, so while the hired orchestras, first one, then another, played Gypsy melodies around Milano's casket, his family and friends kept vigil. Flowers too filled the room, so many that some sprays had to be left in the outer vestibule.

On the second day of the wake, the day before the body was taken to the Russian Orthodox Church for funeral services, the Third Day Black Feast Table-of-the-Dead was set up right there in the funeral parlor in full view of Milano's open coffin. It is called the Third Day Black Feast because it's held three days after death. To begin the Black Feast, one relative close to the deceased stepped up to Milano's cold remains and offered the feast to him.

"Milano, we have set this table for you. We will eat with you here, and also there too, in your world." With the exception of potatoes, because they are grown beneath the ground; onions and peppers, considered vegetables of the devil; and shelled peanuts, each shell being symbolic of another casket, the Black Feast Table was set with the best foods money could buy. More flowers adorned the lavish spread.

On the third day of the wake, close relatives, acting as pallbearers, lifted the closed casket into the hearse. Once in the church, the casket was again opened. During the service each mourner went up the center aisle to place folding money in the coffin by Milano's side so that, if necessary, he could buy his way into heaven. Then the priest closed the casket for the last time.

The procession of cars was so long that a police escort had been requested. Tradition calls for the mourners to walk the last three blocks before reaching the place of burial and so it was for Milano's last journey as all the Gypsies parked their cars to form the procession. The pallbearers with the coffin went first, then came the orchestra, playing, followed by the rest of the Gypsies. At three different times during the funeral march, the customary full stop was commanded by one of the leading Gypsies.

Once at the grave, after the flower-topped coffin was lowered, the mourners threw handfuls of dirt on top of it, along with flower petals. Many men also poured wine and whiskey into the grave, pouring in the form of a cross. Then caterers arrived with sandwiches, soda and beer, and we remained in the cemetery for two hours.

With the funeral over, the mourning continued. On the ninth day, another Black Feast Table-of-the-Dead was held in a rented hall with everything the same as the first Black Feast. At the sixth week Black Feast there was an added ritual. A man was chosen to be dressed in Milano's memory. He was given as much money as needed to buy a complete new wardrobe to clothe himself from head to toe, for he was to sit at the head of the six-week Black Feast Table-of-the-Dead in Milano's seat.

Three Gypsies accompanied him on the buying spree. The companions for such an excursion must always total an odd number, but never just one. Other Gypsies purchased for the chosen man a new towel, washcloth and soap to be used before he ate. In front of him on the table was a new place setting of china and silver flatware, and he was given a wallet filled with money. For the one-year Black Feast, another man was chosen to be completely outfitted in this way. After this feast, the two men took the clothes and tableware to the country and left them for strangers to find.

If a Gypsy's life is cut short as Milano's was, he is mourned for one year. Those close to him refrain from social life and wear black. If a Gypsy dies with a long life behind him, the mourning period ends at the six-week Black Feast.

The last Black Feast table was set one year to the day after Milano's death. As at the six-week feast, and according to tradition, there was an odd number of people present, for we consider odd numbers to be lucky, even numbers unfortunate. The candle ritual was also observed at these two gatherings. With burning incense on a large cooking spoon, a man walked around the table three times before the food could be eaten while everyone stood, the chairs pulled away from the table to allow the incense carrier to move around freely, warding off the devil. Then everyone sat down and two men passed out lighted candles giving the first one to the Gypsy dressed in Milano's memory. The men, walking parallel to each other down the long table, spoke Russian holy words as they handed a candle to each mourner. Each of the 201 people at the table placed his lighted candle in a bun and began to eat. To break the mourning, red soda, cherry, strawberry or grape; beer or whiskey was spilled on the floor in the form of a cross. Although none of the Nickels family attended Milano's Black Feasts, we heard that at the last one the cross was poured in wine and he could rest in peace. So the Gypsy custom continued, and all left over foods and flowers were removed from the hall and taken home to be enjoyed later.

Chapter Seven

Because of their nomadic life, Gypsy children generally attended school—if at all—for only a few months a year. But around the time we were growing up, this changed drastically. Laws were passed that required all children to attend school, so formal public education was added to Gypsy life. Children still continued, however, to receive instruction into Gypsy custom and tradition at home. It was, and still is, the duty of Gypsy parents to teach their children about their heritage and history.

Hundreds of children, unaccustomed to being together in such numbers, are bound to get out of control, and that was the case in our encampment in Sacramento. We ran freely around the campsite and the countryside. As much out of boredom as from mischievousness, a small

herd of us stormed through one of the neighboring
farms, stamping across the watermelon patch. Not a
melon remained whole. When our parents found out,
many of us were reduced to tears, and unable to sit down
for a while. Not only were our parents duty bound to pay
the farmer for his loss, but the incident brought matters
to a head.

School authorities sent a truant officer to investigate
the situation at the camp. He came on several occasions,
each time demanding that the Gypsies conform to the
law by sending their children to school. The men were
afraid, however, that the Gypsy traitor would kidnap
some of the children, holding them for ransom. Everytime we children saw the shiny official car of the truant
officer, we would run into the woods and hide. Our parents had instructed us to do this, but it was more a
delight than a duty. Official warnings continued for more
than a month until one day when a little girl wasn't
quick enough to hide. The truant officer grabbed her and
with intimidating tactics was able to get her name and
those of her parents. That week her parents were summoned to court and fined fifty dollars. The next day the
truant officer brought an army of police with him. Mov-
ing methodically from tent to tent, they wrote down the
names and ages of each family member.

On Monday of the following week, the Gypsy school-
age population, from over 300 tents, attended for the first
time the public school, four miles away. Angelo felt that
we would be safe there and displayed his confidence by

sending my two sisters and me. The other two children were still too young. Even though Uncle Frank was married, he went too because fourteen was still considered school age. Most of the children walked to school while a few trucks traveled slowly along with us as a safety precaution. Taking turns, three men at a time stood guard in the schoolyard, waiting for us to come out. During the four-mile hike, which began at five in the morning, we ate our breakfast on the way, picking oranges and figs from the trees near the road.

With so great an influx of children all at once, the school had to improvise to fit all of us in. Some were mixed in with the *gadjo* children but most of us were tutored in the school basement which was being utilized specifically for our benefit. One month was to be the extent of the Nickels children's schooling because we would soon be breaking camp, but most of the others stayed much longer. It was an exciting experience for all of us and we were eager students. That *gadjo* teacher loved us with a truly caring heart. During that one-knowledge-packed month I learned to read and write, a foundation which has served me all these years.

Chapter 8

Except for the ever-present threat of the Gypsy traitor, the calm California countryside was our oasis of peace away from the outside world. But soon the wedding and its festivities were over, their excitement no longer acting as an eraser for the thought of what could catch up to us from Chicago. And since the children were now in school, many of the men in the encampment, including Angelo, thought it was time to decide what to do about the Gypsy traitor. No longer could they evade his menace. It was there all the time, the fear hovering over them relentlessly.

Angelo and Frank, along with the heads of all the other families, gathered in the center of the campground for what was to be a significant meeting. There were over three hundred men present to hear what their comrades had to say and to offer suggestions as to what could be done to restore once again the confidence and free movement of their people. Protective measures had to be taken to provide for the ongoing life of the Gypsy community.

Frightening stories of the ruthless tough guy and his detestable tactics were told as one man after another stepped to the center of the group to speak his piece, some even repeating threats they themselves had received. One man warned that the Gypsy traitor had ordered his soldiers to hunt down, regardless of where he was living in the United States, any Gypsy who had saved more than $5,000, often the accumulation of a lifetime. Threats of mayhem and murder, used to harass the Gypsies, were also reported, as were accounts of children who had been kidnapped and held for ransom until the demanded amount was paid. As the traitor extorted money from the Gypsies, it was said, he would then turn around and offer a coin or two to the poorest Gypsies seeking to employ them as spies.

One especially well educated Gypsy, acquainted with legal procedures, told those around the campfire that the Gypsy traitor had rolled up more than one hundred and forty arrests for everything from stealing an automobile to murder. "Just imagine the money paid out to lawyers and bail bondsmen to keep his and his henchmen's hides out of jail."

Even though they knew that at present there was no easy solution to the problem of the renegade, many of the men stepped forward to raise their questions and voice their fears.

"How long can we live on the run, in terror like this?"

"There are thousands of us, only one of him. Let's get him," one man cried out.

"Gathered here together, we will starve without income. What can we do?" asked another.

The thirty-year-old Angelo, feeling the hysteria building up, raised his arms to calm the crowd. "All for one, and one for all," he shouted. A thunderous roar of agreement arose from the crowd. "We will not panic," he added, and was echoed by the group of men gathered around him.

Then many ideas for self-protection were discussed, some quite practical, others rather farfetched. But what actually was accomplished was the establishment of a central fund, out of which a lawyer would be hired to insure legal protection should the Gypsy traitor invade California. Each family was to contribute $100, two-family tents $200, and three-family tents, $300. One Gypsy quickly brought out an empty ten-gallon wine jug and stood there checking as each man filed by, stuffing money through the narrow neck of the jug. When the money was counted, the collection came to $50,000.

Since many in the community did not trust each other—$50,000 was a fortune at the time—a group of forty

Gypsies descended on the small law office of the nearest attorney. Unaccustomed to such a crush of people and utterly flabbergasted, probably by their colorful garb, the lawyer insisted that the mob leave his office and send back a few appointed delegates.

But with distrust in their hearts, some with greed, the men found it impossible to select their representatives. They returned to the camp disgruntled and dissatisfied. The money remained in the jug for two weeks, a great temptation to many who were in dire need and down to their last coins. Arguments broke out.

"We don't need a lawyer. We're not afraid of the traitor any longer," said one angry man as he marched some of his followers into the tent where the jug of money was kept. Using a hammer, he cracked it open, knocking the neck off. First his men, then the rest of the encampment came with eager palms up to receive their donations back.

From this incident, Angelo realized the hopelessness of trying to band the entire community together in a single unified body. To make things worse, the local authorities were becoming oppressive. If they saw Gypsies walking down the street, they would pick them up and take them in for questioning. If there was a robbery in the area, Gypsies were brought in and detained, sometimes as long as seventy-two hours, until the real culprit was arrested. Angelo decided it was time for us to break camp and move on.

Our next destination was not planned. At first we moved further into California toward San Francisco. The weather-beaten faces of Angelo, Ruby and Sora reflected the hardships of the past three years which had taken their toll, in body and in spirit. We children had also matured. Gypsy children seem to be born for old shoulders. Although just eight years old, I was ready to tackle any man's job that was given to me. In all, the trip had toughened us, made us a still closer family.

One Monday morning we joined up with another caravan of Gypsies. After traveling about four miles with them, Angelo suddenly turned around and said, "My family, we are going home, back to Chicago where we belong. I'm tired of running. We will do our fighting alone if we must." Everyone cheered. Angelo pulled the car out of line, made a U turn and headed in the opposite direction. Several times I turned around, watching the caravan fade in the distance. We were leaving behind a rootless way of life.

Although Angelo was proud of his Gypsy heritage and wanted us to be proud too, he wanted a better life for us than the one he had known. He believed this could be accomplished by integrating his family into American ways and by earning a steady income. He could do neither while the family was wandering.

In the months to come, freedom was uppermost in everyone's mind. Several times we met other Gypsy families who were on their way to California. Angelo would plead with them to follow us, to return to fight for what was rightfully theirs. But they were too frightened and he was unable to convince them. They went their way and we went ours—and ours was usually quite scenic! Angelo rarely took a direct route anywhere. If a countryside struck his fancy he would follow it to wherever it took us. We lived off the land and often Angelo would drive all night, the junior members of the family sleeping like a litter of pups, piled snugly on top of each other.

On our way through the southern part of Wyoming, we set up camp in a beautiful wooded area along a running stream. We spent nearly a week there because Angelo was making repairs on our Cadillac. One day I left the camp and walked along the water. To my delight, after about two hours, I came upon a peculiarly dressed boy, fishing. A twisted brown scarf circled his head, holding down his black, shoulder-length hair. Both his trousers and sleeveless vest were made of doeskin, fringed and beaded. Having never seen an Indian before, I thought he was a very strange sight. But in a friendly way he motioned for me to sit with him. For the longest while, as embarrassed boys will, we said nothing. Then I spoke up. "My name is George. What is yours?

"Rabbit Hawk." With that he pulled his rod from the water, picked up the fish he'd caught and stood up. He again gestured to me to accompany him and we walked further on. He too must have been lonely for friendship, for the next thing I knew he had cut his right wrist and mine. He placed his wrist on mine and our blood mingled. Then we walked back, tarrying as boys will, to where Rabbit Hawk had previously been fishing. Here he untied his dark brown horse which was barebacked except for a plaid blanket. How I wanted to ride that horse, but I didn't ask Rabbit Hawk.

The three of us walked back to his family's camp. Meat was browning on the fire. Rabbit Hawk's mother, Crescent Moon, sober-faced, hair braided, was tending it. Night Eagle, his father, was smoking a long pipe, the handle of which was colorfully beaded. The smell of the pipe tobacco, as I recall it, was awful, sweet and sickening.

Both Crescent Moon and Night Eagle were also clothed in doeskin, Crescent Moon ornate with a four-strand choker of beads and seven more strands hanging. Night Eagle's ears intrigued me because he wore two sets of earrings, one in his lobes, the other set in the outer edge of the center part of his ears. Their dark yellow tent looked different from those of the Gypsies, and their heavy woven mats were strawlike and didn't look comfortable.

Oblivious to both of us, Rabbit Hawk's parents muttered to one another as we ate from pottery dishes. After the meal, I told Rabbit Hawk I must depart and I thanked his parents who still paid no attention to me. Rabbit Hawk and I left the camp clearing and he helped me up behind him on the brown horse. On the way back he asked me if I had enjoyed his mother's roast dog. Suddenly I didn't feel well.

Angelo and Ruby were relieved and surprised when we rode into our clearing and eager to hear all about my adventures, For the rest of the week the Nickels children had a friend. Rabbit Hawk came to visit everyday and we took turns riding his horse.

Pushing on, we made camp in Nebraska with another tribe of westbound Gypsies, twenty-one tents in all. Since it was a large group, and we yearned for social contact, we stayed with them until they decided to break camp. On our fourth night there, after we were bedded down, someone tugged at our tent.

"Ruby, Ruby, come now, please, it's time," whispered the man. Angelo told us to go back to sleep, that Ruby was going to help one of the women have her baby.

For the longest while, we could hear sudden bursts of loud moaning and painful crying piercing the silence of the night. We also heard whispers that became louder and louder. Ruby was angry with Brunio, the father-to-be.

"Your wife is having difficulty. I can't take on this responsibility. Rena needs a doctor."

"You said you knew how to do it. Ruby, you must deliver my baby. You do it, no doctor!"

"No, she needs medical help. You must get her a doctor, you must."

"I haven't enough money, Ruby. We need what little we have." Ruby looked over at her husband. We didn't have much more than Brunio.

"Angelo, give Brunio five dollars. You take the money for Rena. Now hurry. Get the doctor." Rena was crying out again and Ruby ran to her. An hour passed. Ruby was in and out of Brunio's tent, in and out of our packings, getting things, asking Angelo if Brunio had returned. Two hours later Brunio drove back into camp alone. In his hand, as he merged from the car, was a bottle of whiskey.

"Where is the doctor? Why have you come back with no help?" Ruby asked.

"You do it, Ruby. You deliver my baby." Brunio was drunk. Angelo ran over to him and began to beat him, calling him a spineless pig. Rena cried out again. Ruby motioned to another woman and they went back into Brunio's tent. Everyone remained quiet as Rena's cries became more frequent. Then we heard it, a tiny cry. Another Gypsy, a Gypsy boy, had been born. Rena and Brunio named him John, then Rena, exhausted, slept most of the following day. Angelo congratualted Brunio, at the same time apologizing for the black eye he'd given him. Brunio gave back the five dollars and all was forgiven. There was new life to celebrate.

It was late afternoon and the joy of the new baby still embraced the entire camp. An old Gypsy woman in her eighties was tending the cooking fires. Hungry, I stood by her, hoping for a handout. We were talking together while she stirred the stew when out of nowhere appeared a white-robed man with a beard, wearing sandals. Hospitably, the old woman handed him a hot potato. He ate it at once as if it were cold. He uttered not a word. We watched him in silence, amazed that he could eat red hot food. Then she handed me a piece of bread with hot meat on it. When I looked up, the man in the white robe was gone.

"Where did he go," cried the old woman. No one else had seen him, but realizing how upset she was, several men went out to look for him. Of course, no one found him.

That night the old woman visited me while I lay on my pillow bed.

"My son, little Gypsie George, you and I have shared something very special today. Do you know why no one could find the bearded man? It was because he is Jesus Christ. How special you are. Surely you will be a blessing to our race. You are protected so."

"And you too?"

"Soon my time will come to be with Jesus. I believe this in my heart. My bones ache and I'm tired, but you, George, must always remember our vision."

What I also remember of our Nebraska camp is the fun that we had. Gypsy ball games filled much of our time. These games were played with bats, actually branches of trees, and a handmade two-sided wooden cone shaved blunt on both ends. With two teams playing, the cone would be hit into the air, the object being for one team to get the cone to their base 300 feet away. The game was similar to ice hockey, except that it was played in the air rather than on ice.

Slingshots were another important element in our games, especially when we pretended we were hunters, stalking wild animals. Uncle Bill was the expert at making slingshots and even though we had to pay him a dime to get one made, it was worth it. Uncle Thomas, about fifteen at the time, made car buggies out of crates and wheels. We never knew where he got his equipment, but the buggies even had headlights that lit up, two tin cans with candles set in them. He made one or two every time we set up camp and then sold the creations to local willing buyers. Mechanically inclined, he also developed short oars, rigged with wires on hinges, which allowed a boat to be rowed in the opposite direction without changing the oarlocks. Thomas had an ingenious mind and a fat purse. Gypsy boys always have something to sell.

Chapter Nine

To all of us, being back home in Chicago was an almost indescribable feeling. As we drove down the familiar streets again, we were simultaneously excited, happy, a little nostalgic for our campsite in California, relieved to be home, and a bit anxious as to what the future held for us.

We rented a marble-stepped storefront on the 6200 block of South State Street, and almost at once Angelo ordered a telephone. Because he did not have an established credit background, the only kind of phone he could get was a pay phone. Back in those days, it cost a nickel to make a call. Every so often a company man would come with his keys to unlock the box and collect the money from it.

Two buildings away to our left, Sora rented another store, one with wooden steps. Uncle Frank and Ann, Uncle Bill and Uncle Thomas lived there with her. Grandmother Sora now began to teach the ways of prophecy to Ann. In their front room, as in ours, a portion was sectioned off to serve as the *ofisa*. This curtained-off area was decorated especially for confidential readings with embroidered hangings of symbols and glyphs. Everyday life went on in the rooms behind the store.

Things soon returned to the way they were before our exodus. Angelo went back to working as a coppersmith and Ruby, Sora and Ann told fortunes to eager *gadjos*. Arrangements were made to re-establish a summer booth for them at White City Park.

Sora hardly had her curtains hung when a bald-headed *gadjo* man entered her *ofisa*. His problem, he told her, sheepishly pointing to his almost hairless head, was one of embarrassment. Sora told him to return the next day. That night the women got together. They cut leaves into a deep pot, added dried herbs and olive oil and sprinkled potassium sulphate and sal ammoniac (ammonium chloride) into the mixture. The pasty substance was then packed into a tea can. The next afternoon the *gadjo* returned. Sora gave him the mixture, along with instructions for its application.

"How much money do you want, Gypsy Lady?"

"Give me whatever you can for the church collection. I never charge to heal a man."

A few months passed and the same *gadjo* returned. We hardly recognized him. His hair was growing in. He brought Sora a box of candy and from then on, he remembered her this way every holiday.

Immediately upon our return to Chicago, Gypsies from all the surrounding neighborhoods began to visit us. The Gypsy network is an amazing communications system. Even in those days, news spread across the United States in less than an hour. So it was no surprise to us that the news of our arrival was so widespread.

Yosa and Hena, their uncle, Ephra, and his brother Drago were the first to stop by and welcome us home again. Ephra and Drago had stood their ground, remaining in Chicago when so many others had been intimidated into leaving. We were all pleased to see these old friends again. Even while the greetings were being exchanged, the women hurried off to prepare Gypsy tea. This beverage, served in a glass with a saucer, is sweetened with honey, with fruit sections added. To drink Gypsy tea, we pour it from the glass into the saucer.

Then Angelo began to fill our guests in on the details of our life during the past three years. Because of the Gypsy network, they knew most of what had gone on. Ruby told them how discouraged Angelo had become at seeing the Gypsy people reduced to a condition of such poverty. There was little if any work for the men, the children ran around barefooted, and our people quarreled among themselves.

Angelo broke into Ruby's description. "Drago, I had to come home to be free again even if the conditions are to be adverse. We have to lead the life of the American Gypsy with roots and work and shoes for the little ones. No Gypsy traitor will ever send me on the run again. Never."

Several weeks went by and we were not troubled by one incident or threatening word from the Gypsy tyrant. Angelo, deluding himself, assumed we were completely free of him. No sooner had he uttered his relief one evening to Ruby when our phone rang. Angelo left the dinner table to answer it in the *ofisa*, but we could hear his side of the heated conversation and he later told us the other side.

"Nickels? Angelo Nickels?"

"Yes. Who's this?"

"I hear from the grapevines that you're back. You missed Chicago. They tell me you're going to fight me. Is that right, Nickels?"

"Listen you dun-of-the-devil, I'm back all right and I'm not looking for any trouble from you. Keep your distance, you hear, you traitor bastard." Angelo banged the receiver down. He began yelling. "That no-good bastard attacked Gypsies on the roads, demanded their money. He even shot them. What more does he want? His men attacked the smaller camps. Women were slapped, scared out of their wits." Angelo slammed his fist against the wall, trying to ease his frustration.

"I know, I know, Angelo. Come. Please sit down."
Ruby soothed. The phone rang again before Angelo got
to the table. He answered it.

"Don't you ever hang up on me again, little man. It
makes no difference to me where you live, but if you
want no harm to come to your children, $10,000 will
keep your entire family safe. Be reasonable, Nickels.
Consider it insurance money. Business is very good in
Chicago."

"That's blackmail, protection money, you snake. For
my family I will kill you first. Whatever I paid you, you
outcast, you'd be back. No. No money." This time Angelo hung up the receiver firmly but quietly. He clutched
at his heart as if to still its throbbing. His face was
flushed, his burning anger reflecting from his usually
smiling cheeks. Again came the strident ring of the
phone.

"You have to be crazy, Nickels. You're afraid. Ten
thousand dollars and that will be the end of it, no more
harassment."

"No. No money. We've been through too much. Send
your best soldiers, we're ready."

"You'd better be, little man." Defiantly, and wanting
his turn, this time the traitor slammed the phone down.

Angelo returned to the table. Ruby, tears rolling down
her face, said nothing.

"What will be will have to happen," Angelo said without expression. He was already resigned to what the future might have in store.

Dinner ended abruptly. My sister ran to fetch Sora and the rest of the family. No one slept that night. Into the dark hours through dawn, protective measures were discussed.

"At all costs, we must hold onto our savings," said Sora.

"All of you, every minute, must watch the children," Ruby insisted.

"Don't you let them out, damn it," Angelo yelled at her.

"What's to say he won't bomb one of our places with all or some of us in it? Safe? How can we be safe?" Uncle Thomas had said it all, all the things everyone was thinking. From then on, fear gripped every day and every night.

Chapter Ten

A few months rolled by. Although the Gypsy traitor made no further demands for protection money, we couldn't throw off our sense of unease.

Unlike the American *gadjos*, we Gypsies slept right on the floor on pillows, large feather-filled casings sewn by Ruby. Before God had whispered, "Good morning," around 5:00 A.M. one Tuesday, everyone was suddenly awakened by a thunderous repeating noise. Glass was breaking and bullets were hitting the floor and the walls.

"Stay down, everybody. Stay down for your life," Angelo screamed at us. "Don't raise your heads, we're being shot at." On his belly, Angelo was squirming furiously to reach his gun in the drawer. Ruby meanwhile pushed us together, pulling at our pillows, trying to lie on top of all of us.

As the shooting subsided, the noise of running feet could be heard retreating further and further into the distance. Then we heard car doors slam and tires screech as the attackers made their getaway. Angelo ran outside, gun in hand, firing down the street, but it was useless. By now, everyone on South State Street was outside watching the two cars speeding away.

Ruby telephoned the police. Everyone dressed quickly. A few minutes later the police arrived. Angelo did all the talking, telling them what had happened, pointing out the damage.

"I know who is responsible. It was the Gypsy traitor, he told them emphatically. One of the police officers wrote down everything Angelo told him and then the two policemen departed. The Gypsy traitor was picked up at his home and placed under arrest.

After ordering new glass for the windows, Angelo and Ruby attended the arraignment held late that afternoon. The culprit was required to post bail for his temporary release while he awaited the indictment proceedings. But where legal problems were concerned, the traitor was a seasoned artist. Through masterful manipulation, including the use of payoffs, he could extricate himself from any situation. And sure enough, when the date set for his court appearance rolled around, the traitor had an airtight alibi. This weasel proved, to the court's satisfaction, that he was home, asleep, at the time the shooting had occurred. He was set free, the result of buying off the authorities, Angelo, who was depressed but not surprised, believed.

Despite our anxieties and the interruption of our routine, Sora and Ruby were busier than ever at the amusement park. On several occasions, we had seen another Chicago Gypsy walking around the park, sometimes gaping in the booth with a sickening smile. We found out he was a Mexican Gypsy named Antonio. Angelo became suspicious of him when he began wandering up and down our street, then walking slowly past our two stores. Once he stood right outside the door, leaning against the building, whistling and smoking a cigar.

Several days later, he played his hand. He knocked at the door, asking to see Mr. Nickels. Ruby showed him in. He refused the chair she offered, insisting on standing. Angelo came out into the *ofisa*.

"What do you want? Why are you watching my businesses? You are traitor-bought. Right, Mexican?"

"My friend, I have been sent by our protecting king. All he wants is to take care of you and your family, but protection costs money. You understand. I know you do. Pay him the $10,000. Do yourself a favor."

"You go back, you Mexican slime. Tell that King-of-the-toilets he wastes his money sending fools to threaten the Nickels family. No. No money. Not one blessed cent." Ruby had already opened the door and Angelo helped the Mexican make a speedy exit. The man was brushing himself off before he knew what had happened.

"I will report this, Nickels. You'll regret it."

Four days later, in broad daylight, the Gypsy traitor and three of his henchmen drove up and rushed inside.

"Sorry we can't stay, Nickels, we're in a hurry. Do you

have the money ready?"

"No. No money."

The traitor motioned for action. The gangsters riddled the windows with bullets and they left as quickly as they had arrived. Angelo telephoned the police and reported the shooting. Then he called the window installer again. The landlord had made it quite clear that if repairs weren't kept up we'd be evicted.

For the second time because of a complaint by Angelo, the police went to the Gypsy traitor's home. He pretended he had gotten off his bed to answer the door, but the officers had already checked his car and found the motor hot to the touch. They knew he was lying and they arrested him. But it was the same story all over again. When he went before the judge, he proved to the court that it would have been impossible for him to have committed the act he was accused of. He was released again.

Angelo and Ruby yearned for all of us to go to school. It was their dream, but because of the constant threat of danger, we lived under, it was not to be. The traitor's men were everywhere. They watched us all the time and we never knew when they might harm us. We couldn't go to the corner, let alone walk blocks away to school under such constant surveillance. Formal schooling was virtually impossible. Most of our time was spent playing ball, confined to the backyard. It was just another normal playday when I went into the kitchen for a strawberry drink. I heard a strange voice from the front room, a man speaking to my father. He was introducing himself as the local principal. Quietly I remained in the kitchen, listening to their conversation.

"Your son is required by law to attend school. Surely, sir, you want your children to be educated. All the children in this neighborhood, with the exception of yours and the other Gypsy children in the area, are in school. It is my duty to advise you that if you refuse, preventing your children from being educated, you will be fined, even subject to arrest. Now all this is unnecessary, Mr. Nickels."

"Believe me, there is nothing we want more than to send our kids to your school, and I speak for the other Gypsies as well. You must have read in the newspapers about my trouble with the gangsters. They're shooting up my home. Twice already I've had to replace these big windows. My children live under a daily threat of kidnapping. Will you and your school assume full responsibility for their lives? Believe me, we'd like to have them in school."

"No. Mr. Nickels, we can't take that kind of responsibility. It's up to you. I did read about your plight but the school board sent me. In all probability they have no knowledge of the problems in the Gypsy community. Personally, and off the record, I don't blame your decision. Your children's lives must come first. The school board awaits my report. Rest assured I will enlighten them and ask them if they will accept responsibility for your children or if something else can be worked out. I'll be in touch with you as to their decision."

When the principal left, Ruby put her arms around Angelo's shoulders, trying to show her support.

"Ruby, Ruby, even in California we had to guard the schoolyard," Angelo said in a tone of regret. One day he and his gangsters are in New York, next day Chicago, then California. God Almighty, will it never end?" They lay down and I returned to the ball game. We never did attend the local school.

The situation got worse during the next few years, with 1930 probably the darkest. Shortly after my tenth birthday, in April, we were awakened once more by the thunder of machine guns riddling our home. Again the windowpanes were shattered, the pieces lying everywhere. Splinters of glass peppered our flesh. Trained by now for terror, we stayed still until the gangsters' car drove off.

Sora and the family had decided to stay the night with us because she had had a premonition of trouble. Now Uncle Bill, the nearest to the telephone got up from his pillow bed on the floor to call the police. As he rushed for the phone, we heard a screeching of wheels. Simultaneously, a second blast of machine gun bullets came through the now glassless window. Bullets whizzed past, one missing Bill's face by inches. Sora screamed out his name. Another bullet lodged in the bookshelf immediately in front of him. His expression was frozen in fear. Ruby pulled at his ankles to bring him down to the floor. He would not move. He could not. Shock had temporarily paralyzed him. But in a second or two he snapped out of it and dove for the floor, forgetting to call the police.

Angelo had been checking to see if any of us had been wounded, calling out our names. One by one we answered as we had been rehearsed. Everyone was still on the floor, hearts pounding in sheer relief. All quiet on the street, Angelo permitted us to get up. He looked down at his mother Sora's bed pillow and fell to his knees; bullets had ripped it open, one inches from her side, another above her head. She had told him earlier in the evening that she and the family would feel safer bedding down with us.

There seemed to be as many holes in our walls as there were stars in the sky. We even found a bullet lodged in a chair leg. Angelo began digging that bullet out with a knife as if there weren't more important matters to attend to.

Ruby stared at him. "Angelo?" she said questioningly.

As though in a trance, Angelo headed for the telephone. He wasn't sure what to say, even what to think as he dialed police headquarters. They hadn't helped thus far. Would this be another fruitless call? His heart was numb from the pressure of concern. How long would heaven continue to protect their lives? How long would they be smiled upon? Right now everyone was watching for his assurance, his leadership. He refused to be defeated by the Gypsy traitor. He would not let his family be harmed.

Regaining his usual steady composure, he began speaking to the police. In a few minutes they arrived, took a report, and that was the end of it. The complaint was never acted on. That night we slept at Sora's because the glass installer could not replace the panes of glass until the following day. For hours the women swept, scrubbed, and picked splinters of glass from our pillow beds. Sora prepared a dinner of stew and dumplings in her kitchen, sure it would pump life back into all of us.

Through the network, the neighborhood Gypsies heard what had happened and they vistied us in full force. Angelo's cousin Pete Young, Drago, and the other men huddled in Sora's *ofisa*. Somehow, someway a show of support had to be made. Angelo was unanimously declared their leader. Pete Young volunteered and was chosen to be his bodyguard and runner. Pete was a maverick Gypsy with underworld connections of his own, but he was trusted by Angelo and the others. We were going to fight fire with fire now that Pete was behind us. "If you go down, I'll be beside you," Cousin Pete swore to Angelo.

Angelo had been chosen and his orders would be obeyed because of his courage in standing up alone to the traitor and because he knew the situation better than the others and he knew it from all sides. His selection was an open declaration of their confidence in him and it lifted his heart. "Whatever you decide, we will do," promised Drago. The others shouted their agreement.

Later I overheard Angelo telling Ruby, "So, I am to be the South Side leader. Our people think we have magic blankets because we survived the shooting unhurt; like cats we have nine lives." A lonely chuckle was shared in the midst of a tense atmosphere. Despite our other troubles, we truly were blessed. We had parents who loved each other dearly.

For a few days things were quiet. Sora, Ann and Ruby even ventured outside one day to get a breath of fresh air and hash over the latest gossip. One of the young Gypsy girls, Margie, had run off with a *gadjo*, Harry the Greek. The whole Gypsy community was shocked. Virginity and keeping the blood lines pure are sacred issues and part of the reason Gypsies marry so young. Margie was now an outcast forever. Harry didn't want to marry her but the parents on both sides insisted. Although a disgrace to her own people, she was nevertheless accepted by the Greeks. After dinner that night, my younger sisters were told the story of Margie's plight in warning tones. Ruby's message was "Take heed, remember you are Gypsies, girls who will produce more Gypsies."

It must have been around 3:00 A.M. when we were awakened by a loud knocking, more like banging, at the front door. Everyone remained flat on the floor.

Angelo called out, "Who is it? What do you want? It's the middle of the night. Go away. I'm calling the police."

"Open this door, Nickels."

"No. Go away. Stay away. I'm calling the police."

"You've got three seconds, Nickels. If you don't open it, we'll break it open for you."

Cautiously I got halfway up, craning my neck just enough to look out through the corner of the front window. There was a dark green sedan parked in front of our place. Two men were sitting in the front seats. From my ccorner I was unable to see who they were or how many were knocking on the door. Suddenly the knocking and banging became kicking and my courage vanished. I slipped back onto my belly, burrowing into by bed pillow, trying to disappear beneath the precious security of my knitted blanket.

it was already loaded. Ruby's eyes were glued to him.

"Angelo, what are you going to do, kill him? Oh, my God, save us." She was praying under her breath, half choking on the words.

"Ruby, be quiet and stay down. All of you, stay down."

The banging continued. "I'm going to shoot. I must," Angelo declared. He stood straight in front of the door, his .30-.30 rifle perfectly aimed. Then he fired through the door. I have never heard a man scream so loudly in pain!

Then we heard doors opening and the scrambling of feet as the two men from the car rushed to assist their wounded companion. He continued screaming as they dragged him into the car and sped away.

As Angelo put his rifle away he told Ruby how afraid he had been that Sora and the others would hear the commotion, come out and be attacked. Just then Sora and Frank did‿rush through the door to see what all the banging and shouting was about. Angelo simply pointed to the door. Since nothing more could be done, we bedded down again for a little more one-eyed sleep.

Morning was announced with more knocking on the front door. It was two plainclothes men.

"This is the police. Nickels, open up. Police here."

We were hardly strangers to the police department by this time. They had hurried to our house so many times with only three or four minutes standing between our trouble and their speedy arrival. Ruby quickly opened the door. In a friendly manner, the detectives told Angelo to take his time. They were in no hurry. They'd wait until he had breakfast if he so desired. Ruby made coffee for everyone.

"We're sorry, Nickels, you're wanted down at headquarters for questioning, whenever you're ready."

While the four of them carried on a hushed conversation over coffee, we youngsters were given sweet bread and sent out to the backyard. I overheard their conversation though.

"Nickels, what the hell happened here last night? There's a guy lying in the hospital with a gunshot wound yelling Gypsy Nickels did it."

"The son-of-a-bitch tried to force his way in here. I had no Goddamn choice. Do you guys think I want this traitor war? It's peace we pray for. Look at her, look at my wife. They're killing her day by day."

During the interrogation at the police station, it was

explained to Angelo that he had not directly inflicted the man's wound. The bullet had ricocheted off the front cement walk and bounced back, wounding him in the calf of his leg. Angelo gave the police a full report, his version of what happened. When the questioning was completed, the two detectives escorted Angelo to the hospital and the second floor bedside of his victim. There they permitted Angelo to question the man in his own behalf.

"Why? Why did you try to break in? Who sent you? Look at you, laying there half-dead. Does that Gypsy traitor pay you that well?"

Turning his head as if to turn off his ability to hear, the man remained silent. The detectives could get nothing from him either. A nurse appeared, insisting enough was enough, and they left. Angelo was instructed to appear before the judge at a private hearing.

After the hearing was completed, before dismissing him, the judge confided to Angelo, "Anytime anyone tries to forcibly enter your premises, and especially in the wee hours of the morning, you have a right to self-defense, a right to the privacy of your four walls. Let me give you a little advice. Forget that rifle of yours. Get yourself a better weapon."

"What do you suggest?"

"A Colt .38, like those used by the F. B. I." They both chuckled at the irony of the conversation. To this day, I cherish the revolver Angelo bought at the judge's suggestion.

The police liked and respected Angelo. And thanks to

the newspapers and their coverage of every incident, he was gaining a reputation of leadership. But by this time, Sora was exhausted from worry. Worn out and at her wits' end, she decided a consultation of family heads was in order. She would speak to Angelo. When Sora spoke, everyone listened. Many Gypsies were intimidated by her, so commanding was her presence.

"Angelo, this is getting worse. Machine guns, shootings, next thing we know they'll be tossing bombs at us. My signs tell me that they mean to kill us. Your power is growing and that is interfering with their protection racket."

"Mother, stay brave. We will remain here, no more running. We've taken our stand. God and time will do the rest."

"Doom hangs over us, Angelo. To hell with the stand. Everytime the newspapers carry one of the incidents, business dies. People go by just looking in, looking in for news."

"I'll kill anyone I have to, but we stay."

"It's bad blood that's mixing. I can feel it. If one of them gets killed, one of ours will be and it won't stop there. The trouble will go on. It will be a vendetta. Think about your young ones."

"I am thinking about them and their future. What will you have me do, woman?"

"Let's leave the country. Please, Angelo, see it my way, maybe go to Canada."

"I'm up to my neck now. I don't want my children

kidnapped. I don't want my family hurt. But if we start running again, we may never stop. What kind of an existence is that?"

"I'm sorry, son. I know a man must lead with his heart."

"Remember the hundreds of our people who watch my lead, mother. It's a responsibility I have. You must realize that." Angelo embraced Sora.

All this time Ruby had remained in the kitchen. When she knew they were finished with their meeting of the minds, she served Gypsy tea.

"If we die, we die together and for all Gypsies." Ruby said it all.

This wasn't to be the last time the free spirit of the Gypsies would be tested.

Chapter Eleven

When I first became aware of the disturbance, I thought it was scratching I heard, or maybe matches being struck. I couldn't be sure. It was the middle of the night, past midnight, when I suddenly awoke to the strange sounds. Then I heard two male voices outside our front door. They were speaking a foreign language I didn't understand, but that I now know was Italian.

I had been sleeping on a pillow bed next to Angelo and I was hesitant as to whether I should wake him. In constant readiness, he now slept with a gun under his pillow. If I roused him with a start, it could easily cause an accident. What to do? Deep inside, a part of me kept insisting I awaken my father. Little by little, ever so gently, I began nudging his shoulder. Finally he stirred.

"What is it, son? George? What's the matter?" Angelo was reaching slowly for his gun.

"Shh, father, there are men outside the front door." Silently, too afraid to breathe, we strained our ears to hear what was being said. Their voices sounded mildly amused.

"White or red? I like pure white. It'll stay clean."

"No. I like the red ones. The color will match."

"You're the boss. Red it is." The voices stopped.

Between our place and Sora's was Bob's Restaurant. Here spies, some of them Gypsies, were known to hang out. Perhaps the voices were coming from there. Assuming this, we drifted back to sleep.

Twenty minutes or more elapsed. There is no way to be certain how long it was before there came a tre-memdous roar that rocked the entire block as if we were having an earthquake. Back in California we had experienced a tremor more than once. Now stunned, panic-stricken, everyone jumped up from the floor, not knowing which way to run or even if we should run at all. Screams became our only emotional release. My sisters and my brother were all crying.

Angelo dashed for the door and opened it, gun in hand. Looking toward Sora's he cried, "Oh my God, not my mother!" He was pale, his face drained of its normal color.

Ruby, come quick, Sora's place has been bombed!" Now Angelo understood the words we had heard. When the men were discussing the red and the white, they were deciding between our white cement steps and Sora's red wooden ones. Of course it would be simpler to plant a bomb beneath Sora's, easier to get under them.

Angelo, still clad in yesterday's clothing because we all slept ready for battle, ran over to Sora's store. Fleeting thoughts clutched his heart. His mother, his brothers, Ann, any of them, all of them might be dead. Some might be under the wreckage, lying helplessly trapped. His mind was tortured. Dear God, don't let them be dead. No, God. No.

One of the *gadjos* yelled to him that they were calling for the police.

In our own place, the blast from the explosion had blown out the windows, once again shattering glass all over the sleeping area. Ruby, counting us for fear she'd lost one, lined us up like baby chicks: my brother, Miller, the youngest; then Mary; Mildred; Helen; and me. Then she quickly herded us out into the middle of the street where she remained with us, dusting and picking slivers of glass from our flesh and clothing. Her cheeks were moist from a few tears which had escaped her control. She kept kissing us, one then another. From where we stood, we heard the shouting of my father. He was standing outside the wreckage, yelling.

"Can any of you hear me? Is everyone all right? Are you alive? My God, answer me. Whatever you do, don't move! You hear me, don't move! More wreckage may fall on you. You've been bombed. It blasted a hole in the front of your place. Listen to me. If you come to the front, you'll fall through to the basement. Don't panic, whatever you do. Mother, are you alive? Mother Sora?"

"Yes, Jesus was with us. We are alive. I'm not hurt," she answered.

"Frank, are you okay?"

"Yes, Angelo, but I don't know which way to move."

"Thomas?"

"Yes, I'm in one piece. The bastards missed."

"Ann?"

"Oh, yes, I'm next to Frank. My head hurts."

"Angelo, I'm all right," offered young Bill, so excited to hear Angelo's voice. He hadn't heard all of Angelo's warnings, though. The place was so dense with smoke there was little if any visibility. Bill began to run out. Angelo heard his movement.

"Don't move, Bill. Listen to me, there's a hole up front, where the *ofisa* was." But it was too late. The unknowing ten-year-old had been swallowed up. He lay dazed and in pain on the basement floor, crying out for help.

"My leg, Angelo, help me, please. My leg, I think I broke it. Get me out of here."

Just then, with sirens blaring, police and the fire department arrived. Newspaper reporters and photographers piled out of their cars, creating even more confusion.

Everyone wanted to talk to Angelo at once. All he wanted was for his family to be rescued. He refused to be interviewed. By now, Ruby was by Angelo's side and *gadjos* were watching over us. Since Angelo refused to oblige the newspapermen, two of them approached me.

"Hey, Gypsy boy, how would you like to have your picture in the paper? What do you say, sonny?" The thought of it, of being special, noticed, excited me. I looked at them quizzically.

"You tell me everything you know about what happened here tonight and I promise your picture will be on the front page of tomorrow's newspaper. What do you say?"

"My name is George Nickels. My Uncle Bill, he's ten, he broke his leg. He fell in a hole. My Grandmother Sora's place was bombed." I pointed to her place. Photographers were already taking shots of it. "That's Angelo and Ruby, my father and mother. Will my picture be in the funny papers too?"

They continued to pump information out of me until we were interrupted by Angelo's command. "George, it's time to go home. No talking," he cautioned.

Frank and Ann followed the ambulance which speedily took young Bill to the hospital. He was right; his leg was broken. The doctor set it and he was released a few hours later. Not one of us forgot to say a prayer of thanks before trying to go back to sleep again. Sora and the family would stay with us until their place was habitable once more.

The front page of the morning paper carried a big spread on the bombing, with pictures of Sora's place. Needless to say, my picture did not appear. I felt I had been tricked, cheated, but I learned a hard lesson in human nature.

The windows of many other buildings on the block had also been cracked or blown out by the explosion, including those of Bob's Restaurant next door. Although the traitor's spies used his place as a convenient lookout, all the children liked Bob. Each day he would pass out yesterday's pies through the kitchen door, often inviting us in, especially if business was slow, for the day before's soup. He was a friendly man who loved children and it was hard to hold a grudge against him because of some of his customers.

The police continued to search for clues all day. Strangely enough, they found another bomb four buildings down the block, in a streetcar barn. We could see no connection with our bombing, but the police suspected it might have been quickly discarded there by the gangsters during their getaway.

Everyone pitched in to help Sora get her place cleaned up. There were tons of rubble to sift through for whatever could be salvaged. The entire front of the store had been blown out. With no windows and no doors, it now resembled an open garage. Shattered glass littered the debris, and working in the interior was like walking on eggs. Truly, it was a miracle that any one of them survived, let alone all of them!

An unforeseen tragedy was to evolve from the very same explosion. In our block, the backyards had no dividing partitions. Only the back property lines and the sides of the end properties on the block were walled in with eight-foot wooden fencing. This arrangement provided a spacious playground for the children. Alone in the twilight with everyone still working in Sora's place, I was clamping my shoes into old soup cans to pass the time. I suddenly happened to look up. To my amazement, I saw a white-clad figure dropping from Bob's second-floor back porch, the railing of which was now hanging over lopsidedly. The plump figure, garbed in long lace attire, smashed into the ground-level cellar doors and continued to fall right through them. I ran through Sora's back door, yelling, "Frank, come quick, an angel all dressed in white just fell from upstairs. It's in Bob's cellar. You better go tell him."

It was Bob's wife. She narrowly escaped death. The blast had shaken the railing loose and when she leaned against it, it gave way. When Bob, Frank and Thomas got there, they also found one of her cats running wildly around the cellar. Bob figured it must have been his wife's arms when she fell.

Shadows of adversity did not play favorites. During the same week, the neighborhood children, Gypsies and *gadjos* alike, were involved in a basketball game. Bob from the restaurant was killing time before he went to visit his wife at the hospital and he had joined in the action. Bill sat on the sidelines, still with his leg in a cast. Among the players were Leo and Gus (Gus's father ran a restaurant on the other side of Sora's place), and the Polish brothers, Joe and Julius.

Thomas hit the ball over the fence. Julius and Joe scaled the fence to retrieve it. Then we heard Joe scream and everybody went over the fence. Julius had accidentally jumped on a steam line in the rear of another establishment. It broke loose, scalding his brother's leg. The owner rushed out, picked Joe up and drove him to the hospital immediately. Joe remained in the hospital for six weeks, and on crutches for six months. Ruby was sure the entire block was jinxed.

Chapter Twelve

The Gypsy renegade's reign of terror was intensifying. By the time Sora's house was repaired, we learned that three other South Side Gypsy places had been hit by light bombs, incendiaries made with phosphorus which produced a brilliant flash upon explosion. Pete Young told Angelo that there were four Gypsy spies in our midst and that these spies visited us under friendly pretenses, even talking to our neighbors. Then they carried our news back to the traitor. However, they didn't get anything of a confidential nature. Angelo and Sora were too cunning for that. Often they purposely gave out misinformation. Angelo ordered Pete to get rid of the spies, whoever they were, bomb them if necessary, run them out of state. But no one was to be killed. Now we were fighting the way they were, bomb for bomb, harassment for harassment.

While socializing one day over a cup of coffee in a restaurant on the opposite side of State Street, Angelo glanced out the window to see a strange man peering through our front window. Angelo ran out, crossed the street, and lunged at the man, forcing him face down on the cement walk. Straddling him, Angelo yanked the man's arms behind him and twisted them. This appeared to be the same man our neighbors had previously described to Ruby, telling her he'd been nosing around the neighborhood for days. Angelo had to make sure and get his message across.

"Who are you? Who sent you?"

"My name is Georgeina. No one sent me. Please, let go, you're hurting me."

"I'm only gonna tell you once. You are leaving Chicago. You have twenty-four hours to get out or you're a dead man. Now get out of here."

Angelo kicked him as he was getting up. One of the neighbors ran over and confirmed Angelo's suspicions. "Yes, that's the same man."

More protection of the right kind, was obivously needed for our family. The next day Angelo hired three detectives from the police department. They stationed themselves on the roof of our building. Barely two hours had gone by when a carful of gangsters, speeding past, opened fire on us. Just as the detectives began returning the fire, another passing vehicle got in their way and the shooting ceased. Meanwhile, the traitor's men sped away.

Like wildfire will, news of the incident and the fact that policemen were stationed on our roof spread rapidly all over Chicago. People came from the cracks of the city—curiosity seekers, gossip hounds, newspaper reporters and photographers. The next day, the newspapers carried the story, with accompanying pictures of our broken windows, on their front pages.

Angelo, armed, followed up his warning to Georgeina by visiting his home the following day. He walked right in, without knocking, and confronted Georgeina.

"I gave you twenty-four hours to leave. Your time is up."

Georgeina stared him down blatantly. Angelo pulled out his gun and shot the shocked Georgeina in the right leg.

"I'll be back tomorrow. You'd better be gone."

Indeed he did return to Georgeina's the following day with four of his bodyguards, sons of his cousins. Two remained in the car to guard the premises while Teidor and Larry accompanied Angelo inside. As is Gypsy custom, no door is ever locked, so their entry was unopposed. Georgeina appeared with a butcher knife in his hand. His eyes warned that he had every intention of using it. Cruelly teasing, he passed the point of the blade back and forth in front of Larry and Teidor's faces, almost touching them.

"Your quarrel is not with them. Come at *me,* Gypsy spy!" Angelo taunted.

"Leave, Nickels, or I'll kill you."

Angelo, further angered by the spy's threat, pulled out a tear-gas gun and shot Georgeina in the eyes. With only a few feet between them, the tear gas badly burned his entire face. He began screaming incoherently. Larry and Teidor pulled at Angelo to get him out of there.

"You got it in the leg and now you got it in the eyes. Two hours, that's all you got. I'll be back to kill you."

As Angelo and the boys were leaving, Georgeina's family came running in. They rushed him to the hospital where the police questioned him and he accused Angelo as his assaulter.

Within an hour Angelo, Teidor and Larry were taken to jail. They were allowed one phone call each. Angelo called his lawyer who advised him to say nothing until he could get there. In the meantime, the lawyer got in touch with Sora. Later that day, the three of them were freed on bail and told to appear in court in two weeks. But Georgeina didn't show up then so the judge had no choice but to drop the charges. The case was dismissed. We later heard Georgeina had relocated in Cleveland, Ohio. No one wondered why.

News began to leak from the traitor's camp that he was hurting financially. Angelo Nickels was on his back constantly, causing far too many problems. The Gypsies were following Angelo's lead now, refusing to pay protection money. What with lawyers' fees and putting up bail for himself and his men, obstacles like Nickels could not be afforded. He had to be gotten out of the way.

A plan was devised by the traitor to get rid of Angelo and his own father, a good, clean-living Gypsy who deplored his son's lifestyle, at one and the same time. The traitor put a contract out on his father and hired an out-of-town hoodlum to do the job. To make it worse, he sent two of his own sons (we are sure they didn't know the reason why) to the Greek Cafe to point out their grandfather.

Later, at his own convenience, the killer shot the old man in the upper chest, near his right shoulder. Amazingly, for a little while at least, the old man survived. Furious that the job had been botched, the traitor took his father to a doctor to be checked over. The doctor put some kind of poison on the wound. The poor old Gypsy died. All of the South Side Gypsy community believed that the doctor was bought by the traitor.

Once again the police came knocking at our front door. Ruby answered the door. They asked if this was 6249 South State Street and the home of Angelo Nickels.

"You know right well it is, but he isn't here."

"Where can we find him, Mrs. Nickels?"

"At our concession at White City Park. He's working on the place. What do you want him for, anyway?"

"We have a warrant for his arrest?"

"For what?"

"Murder."

The detectives went to the concession, picked Angelo up, and took him to headquarters. There he told them he had *gadjo* witnesses to prove he couldn't have shot the traitor's father. At the very hour on the day the shooting had occurred, Angelo had been with two detective friends. They were quickly summoned to the station and substantiated his story. Angelo was released at the hearing.

Next thing we knew, the police picked Frank up for questioning. He was held without bail for six weeks.

We heard that at the old man's funeral the traitor put on his best face, acting as pallbearer, wearing the black arm band, blubbering and blowing his nose. (More than thirty years later, we learned the old man wasn't the traitor's real father but his stepfather.) When all legal measures failed to release Frank, Angelo and his men made an unexpected visit to the traitor's home. Angelo advised him that if Frank was not released immediately, we would dig up the old man and have an autopsy performed. Frank was released the very next day.

Chapter Thirteen

Since the Gypsy renegade was using spies in his continuing harassment of us, it seemed only right to reciprocate. And we desperately needed an inside leak. So in the later part of 1931, Angelo devised a plan to infiltrate the traitor's gang. He called upon Al Reardon, a detective friend of his, to play the all-important role.

It was a dangerous scheme, to be sure. There would be many problems involved and much red tape to iron out just to get the plan operative. But Reardon made it patently clear to Angelo that he looked forward, with anticipation, to the plan and his role of intrigue in it.

To begin with, in order for Reardon to take on the undercover assignment, permission would have to be granted by the chief of police. Reardon set up the appointment and he and Angelo visited the chief with high hopes. Quickly the chief dismissed the idea as a ridiculous one, and dangerous to Reardon as well. Angelo was persistent though, refusing to take no for an answer. He told the chief about the Gypsy tyrant's reign of terror and, in particular, about the bombings. He said he believed the law was dragging its heels in this case. The police owed the Gypsy community protection and they weren't getting it. Finally, after an hour of sometimes heated confrontation, the chief reluctantly said, "Yes, permission granted."

Angelo and Reardon returned to our place for the strategy metting. They decided that Reardon, identifying himself as an underworld figure from out of town, was to hang around the traitor's known haunts, talking to his men, gaining their acceptance. He would let them pave his way to their leader's door. Then he would seek employment from the traitor. Angelo realized the enormity of what he was asking of Reardon.

"It's a dangerous job I've asked you to do and I want you to know how much I value our friendship. We will be eternally in your debt, Al."

"Angelo, say no more. This is my meat."

Posing as Tony Aiello from South Philadelphia, Reardon introduced himself to some of the traitor's soldiers in a coffee shop on Fourteenth Street near Maxwell. He filled them in on Philly underworld happenings that he had learned of earlier from the Philadelphia Police Department.

Within a week a meet was set up in the same coffee shop. The traitor was openly suspicious and he warned Aiello he had better not entertain any thoughts of a double cross or of muscling in on his territory.

"All right, Aiello, I'll give you a few small jobs. Let's see what South Philly can do."

Aiello was turned over to one of the traitor's lieutenants from whom he would take orders.

A year passed. On an average of once a month our place was machine-gunned or otherwise harassed by the thugs. In the meantime, Uncle Bill and I had seen a movie produced by Howard Hughes. In it, some gangsters were attacked by the police. To protect themselves they closed steel shutters across the windows, thus blocking the police fire. As soon as I got home, I told Angelo about the shutter scene, and his eyes widened with an idea. The following day he secretly ordered steel shutters to cover the two front windows.They were completely painted with palmistry advertisements, truly looking like painted cardboard blllboards. We are sure they saved our hides more than once. The glass would still break but the steel sheets kept out the bullets.

Before entering our neighborhood, Reardon always disguised himself the same way. We knew all our visitors were watched because the traitor's men had orders to find out who the movie star character was who was in and out of the Nickelses' places. He wore dark glasses, a large-brimmed hat pulled down tightly over his head, and had an enormous handlebar mustache. Of course it was Aiello, Reardon incognito. He came at least once a week to report.

Then it happened. Aiello got a call from the traitor himself. He had a big job for him. Reardon called Angelo as soon as he could to tell him the good news. "The traitor called me for a meet. He finally trusts me. This is what we've been waiting for. I'll be in touch."

Sitting across from the Gyspsy gangster in the coffee shop just as he had a year ago, Aiello received his orders.

"Wipe out Angelo Nickels. Kill him, nice and clean."

"Hey, boss, that's a tall order. I hear everyone's been trying to ground that cracker for a couple of years. If I do, what's in it for me?"

"Three long ones. Three grand, nice?"

"For that kind of lettuce, you got it."

"Okay. You've probably seen the pig's picture in the paper. He's a short, five-foot, nine-inch, greasy Gypsy, dark mustache. We'll talk details tomorrow."

Reardon was panting as he rushed through our door that night. He looked both distraught and excited. Angelo knew something important had happened.

"Al, what's up, what's the job?"

"You're it, Nickels. I gotta kill you."

"Holy Christ, you gotta contract on me?"

"That's it. You're worth three grand to him dead."

Angelo and Reardon embraced each other. This was what they had been working toward all along, the chance to pin something on the traitor. Surely they would get him hanged for this caper. We children were told to hush and say nothing to Ruby.

"I'm meeting him tomorrow, Angelo, for the final details. Now we really have to be careful."

The following morning, the traitor told Reardon, "Aiello, I've decided you do it your way, but I want an example made of the pig. Then all those bastard followers of his will fall into line.

"How about my three grand?"

"Meet me in the hallway in the courthouse tomorrow at noon. Get the job done tonight."

Reardon knew it would be too dangerous at this point in the game to rush over to Angelo's so he decided to call. Angelo was to meet him in a church in a strange neighborhood. Ruby went with him.

Angelo and Ruby had been in the church for a half-hour before Reardon walked into their pew. He'd been sitting in the back of the church when they arrived.

"Angelo, I'm to kill you tonight."

"Then do it now. Tonight they'll be watching. Don't you see? It's got to be now so they can't trace me or catch you off guard."

Ruby came home alone. She fell into Sora's arms sobbing. "Angelo is dead, Sora," she said. All of us children burst into tears. Word flashed through the Gypsy network that Angelo Nickels, leader of the Chicago South Side Gypsies, was dead. No one had any details.

For three days, a pasty looking Angelo lay motionless in a flower bedecked coffin in our front room for all to view. Hundreds of Gypsies filed by, paying their respects. My sisters, my brother, and I were nearly hugged to death by overemotional women. Our house was mobbed with strangers, many from out of state. Each night Ruby asked everyone except the immediate family to leave.

Police were all over the street for fear all hell might break loose between Gypsy factions, at this highly charged time. Some men were actually crying. Now all hope was lost. Who would lead them? Who else had the courage to stand up to the traitor? Their confidence was leveled by fear because their freedom fighter was dead.

I couldn't cry but I felt bitter, especially about Al Reardon and how he had allowed this to happen. I blamed my father's death on him, yet I said nothing to anyone. It made me proud to see so many mourning the loss of Angelo, but deep in my heart I was angry and I felt helpless. How could I, a boy, kill that traitor, I wondered.

Throughout those three days, Sora and Ruby stood by Angelo's coffin, emotionless, seemingly devoid of feeling. Cousin Pete and the other men of our family ringed the coffin.

On the third day, Angelo in his satin-lined casket was transferred to the funeral parlor where the Third Day Black Feast Table-of-the-Dead was set for him. The orchestra was playing when several of the traitor's soldiers arrived. The music stopped. Hushed silence fell over the room, then Sora began screaming.

"No. Don't let them touch my son. No gangsters are going to kiss my Angelo."

Ruby held her and stared defiantly at the gangsters. Many present were frozen with fear. Cousin Pete Young made sure that none of the traitor's henchmen got within three feet of the coffin, only near enough to see that it was Angelo. Drago decked one who tried to come too close. Two of the men grabbed their comrade under his arms and made a hasty departure.

Al Reardon walked up to the casket and was beginning to lean down to kiss Angelo when I lost all control and screamed at him.

"You leave my father alone. Get out. Get out." I could not measure the hate I felt for this man at this moment. Ruby and Reardon realized the shock I was suffering and they took me into a back room from which coffins are loaded into the hearses. Reardon tried to comfort me. I was terrified by his presence and too paralyzed to speak. Reardon would kill me too, I feared.

Just then the undertakers brought the closed coffin into the room. My heart was grief stricken. The undertaker lifted the coffin lid. Reardon leaned over and kissed Angelo. I thought I heard him whisper something. All of a sudden Angelo sat up and put his finger to his lips for me to remain quiet. Actually, I hadn't a word left in my head anyway.

Ruby and Reardon took me, now in a daze, back to the front room and then outside where the mourners were getting into their cars as their names were called out. Ruby, Sora, Pete, and Frank rode in the lead limousine. Ann stayed with us children. Drago drove our car. Three blocks away from the cemetery everyone left the cars and formed the walking procession. At the cemetery, emotions rose again. Tears flowed and wailing resumed as Angelo's casket was lowered into the freshly dug hole. Two of the traitor's men were stationed in a car a distance away, watching to make sure Angelo was buried. Then we returned home.

Al Reardon had picked up the three thousand dollars from the Gypsy gangster which was all the evidence the police needed to convict him. After the funeral, Reardon and two other detectives arrested the traitor, picking him up in the coffee shop. Angelo came out of hiding and came home. He and Reardon were jubliant. Their plan had worked!

We learned some of the details then and the rest many years later from Pete Young. That day in the church, Al took Angelo out the back door to where his car was parked. They drove up to the North Side of Chicago where Angelo stayed in a hotel with a bodyguard arranged for by the chief of police. When Reardon met the renegade the next day to receive his payment for the "job," the traitor refused to give it to him, saying, "You'll get paid when I know he's in his coffin and buried."

This was an unexpected development, but Reardon and Angelo were not stumped. They soon had ready for display a coffin containing Angelo's "body"—a wax figure with the head made from a casting of Angelo's face.

On the day of the burial, Angelo, who had remained in hiding, said to Reardon, "Al, by now my family's out of their minds with grief. I have to let them know I'm alive."

"Christ, Angelo," Al said, "after all this are we going to blow it now?"

"We have to find a way, Al, "Angelo insisted. And they did.

Angelo was placed in the coffin, which was left slightly ajar, and driven to the funeral parlor. When he was satisfied that his family knew he was alive, he was smuggled back to his hotel and the wax figure was replaced in the coffin and subsequently "buried." The traitor was sure he had seen the last of Angelo and he "paid" Reardon off.

But Angelo's and Reardon's jubilation didn't last long. The traitor was released on bail and he immediately fled to New York. When Angelo heard this he became infuriated. That very hour he hired New York Gypsies to track down the traitor. When they did, and it didn't take too long, Angelo, Reardon, and two other undercover policemen went to New York and brought the traitor back in chains. Not all of the Gypsies believed that the traitor had finally been stopped. This hurt Angelo deeply. He took several of them down to the jail to see for themselves. When the traitor was faced with the group of gaping Gypsies he became violent, screaming and yelling threats at them. The Gypsies left hurriedly, still intimidated by the outcast.

When the renegade came before the judge for jumping bail, he played innocent, telling the court he had no idea he wasn't allowed to leave the state. The court believed him, releasing him with a much stiffer bail. That was the law's mistake and the Gypsies' fortune because the traitor needed money, a lot of it. His luck was running bad. He robbed a bank but one of his own henchmen went to the F. B. I. and fingered him for the job.

As a foul odor eventually dissipated with fresh air, so it was as time and constant resistance dissolved the traitor's power. Caught with one of the hundred dollar bills in his pocket, the Gypsy gangster received a sentence of from four to fourteen years. What feasting and celebrating went on in Gypsy circles all over the states!

Chapter Fourteen

After the traitor was safe behind bars, Angelo decided we had earned a vacation. For a complete change of scene, he decided we would go to France. But at the last minute, with our passports ready, three different Gypsy families talked Angelo out of it, persuading him to go to Canada instead. Many Gypsies had fled there when the traitor was playing hell with our people, and Gypsies follow Gypsies.

True to Angelo's wanderlust we didn't travel directly to Canada. First we detoured to California to renew old acquaintances in the camps there. Everywhere we stopped, Angelo got a hero's welcome. As proof of what he had accomplished, many Gypsies were breaking camp, looking forward confidently to settling down roots elsewhere now that it was safe to do so.

When we drove across the Canadian border, Ruby immediately fell in love with the landscape and the newness of it all. Angelo purchased property but we remained there for only a year. Then we traveled west across Canada, returning eventually to California by way of Seattle, Washington and Portland, Oregon. In the summer of 1933, we arrived in Stockton.

During our stay in Canada, Angelo became friendly with the Frank family and chose a bride for me, their daughter Anushka (Ann) Frank. Following age-old tradition, Angelo negotiated with Ann's father Tosha. Although he was reluctant to have his daughter marry at the time, Tosha recognized Ann's and my affection and friendship and finally agreed that the wedding could take place in a year. Before we left Canada, arrangements were made for the Franks to follow us later. The bride's price was $2,500.

We were married in Stockton, California, in 1933. I was thirteen years old, Ann was twenty-one. Our first son, Steven, was born a year later in New York. When her time came, Angelo and Ruby took Ann to the hospital to deliver the baby. Later I went to visit the two of them but the hospital authorities refused to let me in. "No children allowed in the maternity ward," they said. The *gadjos* knew nothing of Gypsy ways. Angelo returned with me to the hospital, explaining who I was. Finally, I got to see my wife and our son.

Fortunately he was healthy and whole. No pierced ear or gold earring would ever be necessary. Gypsy custom is such that if the first son dies, the second son's right ear is pierced by his mother and she places a gold earring through it. Having damaged his ear she has thus petitioned God to protect his life.

We continued to travel through the United States, settling back in Chicago in 1938. Sora passed away two years later, in her sleep, at peace. There wasn't one of us who didn't miss her strength. Angelo took her loss very hard and mourned her for well over a year.

World War II took its toll of Gypsy lives as well as *gadjo*. Being a man who hated injustice of any sort, every morning's newspaper saddened Angelo more. Through the Gypsy network we heard of a Spanish Gypsy family named Moraz who had been trapped in Poland. Through the underground forces they were aided and later escaped from Europe. They brought with them unbelievable tales of Nazi atrocities against the Gypsies, who were considered even lower than the Jews.

Since the Gypsy way is to give generously in time of need and to befriend all in the race, Angelo visited the Moraz family and assisted them financially. One day Angelo asked Mr. Moraz to tell him what he knew of our people in Europe. At first the old man hesitated, his eyes mirroring the gloom and despair of the European hell. His voice lowered.

"They were herded into cattle cars under the pretense of being resettled. Others were marched away on foot to the concentration camps, the aged, the sick, the children as well. Those who lingered were shot. Our people were worked to death. Turnip soup made of dirty water and bread crumbs were all they were given to eat. When they first arrived at the camps they were stripped bare, given wrong size clothing, thin and ragged.

"At Auschwitz, of 11,000 Gypsies all but 1,500 perished. Guards at the crematoria referred to our people as *Gypsy salami.* Sometimes Gypsies were submerged in water or had rubber tubes forced into their mouths stimulating anguished sensations of drowning. Sadistic sexuality ran rampant. Naked men and women were forced to parade for hours in the bitter cold, in the rain and snow. In one incident I heard of, men were nearly frozen to death, then brought in and surrounded with young women, timed to see how long it would take them to begin to copulate. Gypsy women were compelled to submit to the sexual desires of their captors.

"Prisoners were turned into locked compounds with purposely starved, vicious dogs. Defiant prisoners were forced to stand beneath hoses for hours. Some were tied naked to stakes and coated with honey. Then a hive of bees would be unleashed at them. Corpses were used to manufacture soap and fertilizer.

"We lost at least a sixteenth of our population. Angelo, do you know we are mourning more than 500,000 Gypsies?"

Angelo got up and went over to Moraz, embracing the teary-eyed man.

Angelo continued to work as a coppersmith until he retired in 1950. I worked with him until that time and then I devoted myself to my amusement business on the Jersey shore where we were then living. In late September of 1956, Angelo suffered a stroke and was hospitalized for twenty-one days. During this time, thousands of Gypsies poured into Wildwood, New Jersey, to pay their last respects to the man who was responsible for freeing them from the traitor's clutches. More Gypsies arrived every day, some from as far away as California. Hospital authorities were at a loss as to how to handle the crowd. Most of the concerned simply remained outside the hospital, quietly keeping a reverent vigil. Nevertheless, the police were summoned to maintain order.

"This is our leader dying. We come to pray him away," was the Gypsy reply. On October 17, Angelo died at the age of seventy-one.

The gadjos called him king; our people still call him the Gypsy leader.